No Pants Required

More Craft Cocktails for the Couch

By Tim Harnett

Cover art by Kymm! Bang

Photography by Sara Maresco

Edited by Carol Harnett

CP

Cooperative Press
Cleveland, Ohio

No Pants Required: Craft Cocktails for the Couch

ISBN 13 (print): 978-1-937513-99-3
First edition
Published by http://www.cooperativepress.com

Text ©2023 Tim Harnett
Photos ©2023 Sara Maresco
Editor: Carol Harnett
Cover art: Kymm Bang

Every effort has been made to ensure that all the information in this book is accurate at the time of publication; however, Cooperative Press neither endorses nor guarantees the content of external links referenced in this book.

If you have questions or comments about this book, or need information about licensing, custom editions, special sales, or academic/corporate purchases, please contact Cooperative Press: info@cooperativepress.com or 10252 Berea Rd, Cleveland, Ohio 44102 USA

No Pants Required
More Craft Cocktails for the Couch

CP

Cooperative Press
Cleveland, Ohio

Dedicated to Kingsley Amis, Oliver Reed,

Peter O'Toole, Richard Harris, and all the

other inspirational drinkers that drew me to life at the bar . . .

and eventually a career behind it*.

*(... Add a quiet nod to the Uber drivers who deal with my slurred speech.)

Table of Contents

Foreward

Last year I penned and published my first book—No Beard or Bowtie Required, Cocktails for the Craft Curious. This accomplishment surprised me more than anyone. Not much motivates me, as advancing age, weight and exhaustion fill me with inertia. The unprecedented coronavirus pandemic ironically aided my goal as an author. The bar I work at closed for many months during the lockdown, compelling me to burn what few calories I do typing away on the couch.

Enough people bought it that I decided to suffer for my art a second time. Here we are two years later and said pandemic refuses to expire. Many bars intermittently lock their doors while their weary patrons recede into their living rooms in fear. So here I am, committing as many of my cocktail creations to paper as my sanity might once again allow.

Some industry colleagues took issue with the previous book's title. Many of them had well-groomed beards and mustaches. They often sported bespoke waistcoats and bow ties. It did not condemn these conventions, as much as it said you simply don't need them to execute killer cocktails.

Frankly, I'd carry on the cocktail bar's sartorial wardrobe and grooming traditions and defend them jealousy, if I could. The simple fact remains that this goddamned pandemic lulled me into a 70-pound weight gain that will likely keep the coroner from shutting my fucking coffin lid.

Historically I've suffered attempts at a good beard. Which is truly unfortunate as beards hide double-chins really well. But as of this penning, I've forced out enough facial hair to conceal several chins.

All of these circumstances belie an ongoing dilemma for the discerning drinker. People aren't packing into bars anymore. And many like myself have succumbed to the garb for men of increasing age and girth. The mirror became a greater enemy than excessive drink. You can damn well bet the author photos in this book will be at least four years old.

In that spirit, I give you the guiding ethos of this book: Even if your body gives you elevated blood pressure, a tentmaker's wardrobe, and general unending shame, you can still make very good cocktails at home. Or hell, maybe you want to build out a full bar at home too.

Hence, you don't need pants. You don't even need undergarments. You just need the right tools, good ingredients, and a comfortable seat. Probably a couch. Well-fit people can embrace these tenets too. They'd probably just be more inclined towards coitus after a few good drinks.

So to kick things off—buy my first book or borrow it, if you have not already done so. It covers the proper bar tools, core spirits, and other ingredients that you'll need for proper shaking and stirring. I'd loan you my copy but I really need to sell it to help cover the costs of publishing it.

Seriously. At this point, I still don't think I'm in the black.

Reading onward, you'll find that this book shows off some more specialized tools and ingredients you can play with at home. Some of the tools use open flames, have extremely sharp blades, or other potential perils for the clumsy. I've bled and blistered enough to know that bar-related injuries don't really stop, one just gets moderately better at avoiding them. All I ask is that you do not bleed on the book.

This book also leans more on flavor profiles than the first book. Each chapter takes inspiration from the syrups, juices, and other exotic ingredients that make the drinks so appealing. The first chapter, for example, fully highlights drinks made with orgeat. Friends and guests alike know all too well my crippling addiction to orgeat. I trust you'll become an addict too.

Bear in mind some of the recipes to come call for some fairly eclectic spirits, bitters, and other flavor modifiers. I truly believe this is why the internet exists. Remember, even if your state prohibits shipment of spirits from other states, you'll always find a maverick spirits site that just doesn't give a fuck about your uptight state's booze-shipping laws. It also helps if you live in control states like Ohio, where most of the liquor store shelf space is devoted to shit vodkas.

You'll also find that certain spirits and other ingredients reappear in multiple cocktails throughout the book. This is not accidental. It enables you to get more mileage out of one item, and also see how certain spirits impact the flavor of diverse mixtures.

Also remember this thought as you read onward—the drink garnishes are usually accessible and simple. I've bore accusations of lazy garnishing throughout my bar career. Frankly I think a good drink should be reward enough, and a garnish just provides nice accompanying aromatics. Don't dress up a drink like a southern belle with a fucking Kentucky Derby hat. The garnish usually ends up in the rubbish anyways. You're making a guest wait while their drink gets warm or watery.

Oh yes. And if you favor vodka, just stop reading here.

True believers, read onward. I'll be drinking with you in spirit.

Tim
December 2022

Chapter 1: More Bar Tools and Tricks from the Magic Murderbag

In the first book, I laid out the basic bartending tools you should obtain for any decent home bar. These include a set of weighted Boston shaker tins, a good Hawthorne strainer, a bar spoon, a muddler, and measuring jiggers of your preference. While not entirely essential, a good mixing glass and julep strainer help you execute stirred, spirit-forward cocktails with more panache.

I can't assure that you've picked up "vol 1", so to speak. So let's lay out the key bar tools you'll need around the house:

- A set of weighted Boston shaker tins (18 and 28 oz)
- A jigger of your desired shape, with gradation lines for varying measures
- A high-quality Hawthorne strainer
- A narrow gauge, tight-spiraled bar spoon of your desired length
- A mixing glass with capacity for at least two cocktails
- A julep strainer for the mixing glass

All of these essential tools will fit in a humbly-sized bar bag. I nicknamed my bag the "magic murderbag", after the medicine case of Dr. Henry Killinger on The Venture Brothers. This vessel, like any good bar bag, has enough room for a few extra tools.

Additionally you can seek out some other tools for cocktails with a bit more flair. This book calls for some such drinks. Honestly, I've always strayed away from cocktails that demand all manner of dazzling preparation and over-the-top garnishes. Good drinks already have a waiting period. I have no desire to go to the Aviary and have a cocktail delivered by a balloon that explodes and spreads rose petals over the table.

Sorry, I'll take a Jack Rose for $8 in two minutes over a big city bar tab any day of the week. A good drink is a reward in itself. Who needs a Cirque du Soleil presentation to jack up the price? Go to Benihana for some cheap shrimp if you need a stage show.

And as for you flair bartenders, off you fuck. You might be able to juggle, but you're probably tossing around bottles of stupid flavored vodka.

That being said, some tools let you add some eye-widening touches with minimal effort. Let's start with the atomizer.

Drinks don't call for atomizers too often but it's good to keep them in your toolkit. This perfume-style spray bottle disperses a fine mist or "rinse" over a chilled glass or the surface of a prepared cocktail. You can rinse a chilled glass before a cocktail goes in it, or you can spray a mist over a drink that's already in the glass. Each method results in some pretty dramatic aroma effects.

The atomizer pictured on the previous page is a Jeffrey Morgenthaler atomizer. It has a bigger capacity than most other atomizers and has a better, more reliable misting effect. You can get much cheaper atomizers. But in my experience, the sprayer usually breaks way too soon. This isn't too heartbreaking since you're essentially buying a cheap, empty perfume bottle. But I can more or less guarantee you'll have to get a replacement soon enough.

If you're so inclined, add a smoker set to your bag of tricks. This includes a smoking chamber and smoker gun, a butane torch, and one or more types of wood chips. It adds a layer of aromatic smoke over the glass and the surface of a prepared cocktail. Typically it best suits spirit-forward whiskey drinks (quite popular with old fashioneds). Be warned—once a guest sees you use this contraption, you'll likely be stuck making several more drinks for those who are easily dazzled.

After you make one or more cocktails, place them inside the smoking chamber. Connect the smoker gun hose to the hose port on the chamber (if it has one), or put the end of the hose under the bottom edge of the chamber glass. Add wood chips to the screen in the smoker gun and turn it on. Light the chips until the chamber fills with smoke and then turn off the gun. Let the smoke settle for about 15 seconds and then enjoy your smoked cocktails.

Smoking cocktails does not necessitate a swank smoking kit. You can smoke drinks with a bell jar, a cheap cutting board, and a lighter. All you need to do is light some chips on the cutting board next to the drink, then place the bell jar over the drink. Alternatively, you can get quite fancy kits that have gilded panes of glass. It depends how much you enjoy smoked beverages and how much money and pageantry you want to devote to them.

Smoked cocktails commonly feature citrus peels from oranges or lemons because the citrus oils pair so well with the flavor and aroma of citrus oils and spirits. You can easily peel an unassuming swath of orange or lemon using a y-peeler or even a potato peeler. For some added flair, consider adding a ravioli cutter to your repertoire.

The photo shows an inexpensive ravioli cutter. After cutting your citrus peel, you can cut it into various shapes with the decorative flair of a jagged edge. The peel can also be twisted into different shapes and mounted on the edge of a glass. Check out the photo for a common motif you'll see at good cocktail bars.

I'll level with you—that's about as flashy as I'll get with garnish tools, or other bar tools in general. Being on mailing lists from cocktail tool suppliers will tempt you plenty towards more gear than you need. Be warned.

Chapter 2: Ode to Orgeat
To the Lament of those with Nut Allergies

Orgeat is an enchanting syrup traditionally made from almonds, sugar, and either rose or orange blossom water. Tiki cocktails lean heavily on this syrup, alongside some other classics scattered across the decades. Its versatility led me to most of the tiki drinks I've created over the years. I'll confess a certain reliance on it by this point.

A growing number of small producers make a wonderful array of orgeat syrups today. Some have ventured into other nut bases like pistachio, hazelnut, and macadamia, while also testing new floral waters like pea flower. Admittedly this makes the job of a mixologist much easier. If you make it yourself, the same principles apply; you just make the syrup with a nut variety other than the classic almond.

This chapter sings to my love for a syrup that has almost become a crutch to my creativity. I've defaulted to it to the point of embarrassment. Rather than recoil from that reliance, I say embrace it. It's just too good to reserve for Mai Tais and other tiki sours. Just be patient when people a) try to pronounce "orgeat" and b) ask you what it is every time you use it.

While the variety of orgeats in this chapter carefully add depth to each drink, you can make each one using classic orgeat. All will still taste lovely even if more exotic styles of orgeat are out of reach.

To those with nut allergies, I guess just skip this chapter. Actually, tell a lie, orgeat makes these drinks so good, it's worth a stab in the leg with an epi-pen.

Happily Hellbound

This drink pleases me on so many levels. It spawned from my adventures in tiki. It uses a superb mixing whiskey. And of course it includes the almondy goodness of orgeat.

This cocktail pays tribute to the Godfather of Hellbilly—Elvis Hitler. A living legend in both the rockabilly and punk arenas, he accepted our invitation to perform at several special events. The Hellbilly takes its name from the title of one of his classic songs, and employs his favorite spirit—Wild Turkey 101.

The Hellbilly debuted at a shared 50th birthday celebration for my wife and myself. Elvis drank his out of our speed demon tiki mug. After drinking six of these myself, I probably killed enough brain cells to technically advance my age to 51 in one evening.

The Hellbilly

2 oz Wild Turkey 101 Bourbon or Rye

½ oz Giffard Orgeat

¾ oz fresh lemon juice

½ oz Ancho Reyes

2 dashes Bittermen's Hellfire Shrub bitters

Shake all ingredients with ice and strain over fresh ice in a large rocks glass. Garnish with a mint sprig and fresh jalapeno pepper rings.

Polynesian Pick-Me-Up

When you imagine coffee and orange juice in the same glass, you might wince. Think again. Orgeat and the correct spirit blend connect these two breakfast staple beverages quite harmoniously.

This cocktail also proves the merits of true traditional spiced rum. It will work with something like Bacardi spiced, but better spirits make better drinks. Just avoid Captain Morgan as a personal favor to me. Please. It's the toilet wine of rum, and honestly the stuff of nightmares that I wish I could forget.

Actually if you have Captain Morgan, do yourself a favor and pour it over the grave of a dead enemy. Or use it to waterboard a living enemy.

Kona Kaimana

1 oz craft cold brew concentrate

½ oz Patron Citronge Orange or similar

1.5 oz Chairman's Reserve Spiced Rum

½ oz fresh orange juice

¼ oz Nux Alpina

½ oz classic orgeat

Shake all ingredients with ice and strain over fresh ice in a Mai Tai or large rocks glass. Garnish with an orange wheel and fresh coffee beans.

The Hellbilly (left),
Kona Kaimana

Red, Gold and Green

Pistachio orgeat snuck into the wells at some craft cocktail bars, and being the orgeat addict I am, I took notice. It didn't really hit me until then that it was like "duh, you just make the syrup using nuts other than almonds". Researching pistachios for this book, I discovered a lot of weird shit.

Studies suggest that these delicious yellow and green nuts aid with sleep, kidney function, and male sexual vitality. They can also reduce cholesterol and high blood pressure. On the flipside, too much pistachios can cause gas and bloating.

Sheesh I'm coming off like that ass clown Dr. Oz. Just enjoy this liquid version of the yellow and green nuts. You won't get that red harvesting dye all over your fingers and lips. I must insist that you use the specified peach cordial for this drink. Save that peach schnapps shit for the college kids and their stupid green tea shots.

Stoned and Dethroned

½ oz pistachio orgeat

½ oz Giffard or Tempus Fugit Creme de Cacao

1 oz Pierre Ferrand Peche cordial

1 oz Espolon Silver Tequila

¾ oz lemon juice

2 dashes ginger bitters

Shake all ingredients with ice and strain mixture over fresh ice in a rocks or Mai Tai glass. Garnish with a fresh peach cube on a bamboo skewer.

Born on the Bayou

The next orgeat evolution we're dabbling with is pecan orgeat. El Guapo makes fantastic Creole orgeat using Louisiana pecans, with hints of orange blossom and rose waters. This creation bonds southern US heritage with some tropical flavors that play well with pecans. Cue the Jelly Roll Morton.

Dapper Dan

½ oz El Guapo Creole (Pecan) Orgeat

1 oz Uncle Nearest 1884 Small Batch Whiskey

½ oz Giffard Banane du Bresil

½ oz Nux Alpina or Nocino

¾ oz white grapefruit juice

2 dashes orange bitters

2 dashes El Guapo Chicory Pecan Bitters

Shake all ingredients with ice and strain mixture over fresh cubes or pebble ice in a tulip glass. Garnish with a fresh grapefruit wedge.

Stoned and Dethroned (left),
Dapper Dan

The Butterfly Effect

Butterfly pea flowers have an intensely purple and sweet floral effect on liquids. So when infused into orgeat, you can imagine the impact on this already intently sweet almond syrup. Pea flower takes various forms such as dried blooms, teas, and craft syrups, and flower extract. The syrup can be blended with orgeat to combine flavors, or the flowers can be infused with the almonds if making the syrup yourself. The simplest method to get the floral flavors and vibrant purple color, however, is to blend natural extract like B'lure with the orgeat that you make or purchase.

Orgeat's been shacking up with rum for decades, but this drink adds some Asian elements into the mix—some sudachi juice to counter the sweetness, with a good dose of plum wine to stretch it into a snifter-filling delight. Botanists believe sudachi juice comes from a hybrid of yuzu and mandarin oranges. So temper your citrus choices based on this if sudachi is out of reach.

Blue Valentine

1.25 oz butterfly pea flower orgeat

½ oz Giffard Blue Curacao

1.5 oz Tiki Lovers' White Rum

¾ oz Yakami Orchard Sudachi Juice

1.5 oz Choya Umeshu Japanese Plum Wine

2 dashes clove bitters

Shake all ingredients with ice and strain over fresh ice (pebble, if possible) in a snifter or tulip glass. Garnish with edible flower.

Fizzing Out

Hazelnut blends fantastically with most any form of fruit, particularly banana. Orgeat, meanwhile, makes a mean fizz. So let's make an orgeat fizz made entirely with fruit cordials, yeah? This drink gets its fruit flavors from mango and natural banana cordials, while kabosu juice balances out the sweetness with whispers of mint and melon. Fresh lemon will work in place of kabosu.

Last Mango in Paris

¾ oz BG Reynolds Hazelnut Orgeat

1 oz Patron Citronge Mango cordial

½ oz Giffard Banane du Bresil

½ Yakami Orchard kabosu juice

1 egg white

Club soda to top

2 dashes walnut bitters

Carefully crack an egg and separate the egg white into your shaker. Add the syrups, juices, and spirits. Shake without ice for 30 seconds. Add ice and shake for another 30 seconds. Strain mixture into a Collins glass. Top with cold club soda until full. Drip bitters onto the surface of the foamy drink surface.

Blue Valentine (left),
Last Mango in Paris

It Came from Bollywood

This drink unfolded in a weird way. I wanted to pay tribute to one of Wes Anderson's less lauded films, while pairing up some refreshing flavors that pair well with the light nut flavor of pistachio. What you see here I'd fancy drinking in the bar car of a train traversing the hot railways of India. I'd have gone with Mangosteen, but damn if that isn't expensive and hard to find.

Darjeeling Limited

¾ oz pistachio orgeat

1 oz blood orange juice

1 oz Pierre Ferrand Peche cordial

1 oz plum brandy

2 drops orange blossom water

Shake all ingredients except orange blossom water with ice and strain over fresh ice in a Collins or zombie glass. Garnish with a fresh slice of star fruit or passion fruit and an edible flower. Drip blossom water onto the drink surface.

Queensland Shuffle

The New South Wales and Queensland regions of Australia gave the world macadamia nuts. Did you know that? I didn't until checking google just now.

Anyhow, when conjuring up something to do with macadamia nut orgeat, my mind went straight to the white chocolate cookies in which they have become so popular. But honestly the chocolate liqueurs scare me too much, like I'll accidentally slip into some sweet nonsense "martini" recipe. I really should just scratch out this paragraph.

Coming to my senses, I took refuge in the inspirations of the Trinidad sour, which relies heavily on orgeat and dark bitters. The amped-up sour below brings some of those sweet cookie elements with aromatic and sour components. It also calls for aquafaba to give it the traditional forthiness of a sour. Not a necessity, but it gives it a nice texture with minimal effort.

Shambleton Sour

½ oz macadamia orgeat

½ oz vanilla syrup

1.5 oz wheated bourbon (such as Weller)

½ oz Pierre Ferrand Framboise cordial

¾ oz fresh lemon juice

2 dashes Angostura Cocoa Bitters

1 bar spoon aquafaba

Add all but bitters into a shaker and then add ice. Shake and strain into a chilled coupe. Drip bitters onto the surface of the foam.

Shambleton Sour (left),
Darjeerling Limited

Chapter 3: The Honey Pot
Drinks the Bees Brought Us

The honey bee population seems to drop every year. I guess take advantage of this chapter as much as possible while you can. Bees are vital to the food chain, too. So once they're gone, we'll all be fighting each other for food, water and petrol in an apocalyptic wasteland. If that's not an excuse to drink right now, I don't know what is. Hell, the little bastards have to rip their own ass off if they sting you protecting their hive. That deserves some respect.

Damn, that was depressing. Moving on . . .

Honey probably holds more of a lauded place in cocktailing than orgeat. The Bee's Knees, Navy Grog, Airmail, and several other classics have honey to thank for their ongoing legacy. However, bars vastly underutilize honey in my view. Especially with the plentiful array of artisan honey at your disposal.

Just consider this handful of honey varieties:

- Manuka honey
- Lavender honey
- Heather honey
- "Hot" or pepper-infused honey
- Clover honey
- Wildflower honey
- Orange blossom honey
- Salted honey

Imagine the delicious shit you could do with these varieties alone? Again, everyone will think you're a cockstar (cocktail rockstar—I just made that term up, like right now), while once again getting so many layers of flavor from someone else's hard work. Damn, why am I even giving up the ghost like this? Forget I said anything. Read another book.

Sorry, keep reading. I guess these books only exist by sacrificing trade secrets.

Bear in mind that, while a great deal of thought went into pairing spirits and other stuff with specific kinds of honey, your standard-issue pure honey will work in each of the drinks in this chapter. Each type of honey will need to be made into "mix" with 50% hot water. Otherwise it will be too thick to pour or fully mix into cocktails.

Tasmanian Angels

Manuka honey gains its unique flavor from the native bees of Australia and New Zealand, and by default, the island Tasmania. These fuzzy, winged soldiers specifically pollinate the indigenous tea tree plants. The resultant honey apparently carries with it strong antibacterial and healing properties, but I could give a toss. The shit just tastes good.

You be the judge. Taste some straight when you dilute the honey with a little water to utilize it for mixing. Meanwhile I'll spare you the predictable shire joke, or some dumb quip about a barbie.

Tasman Sea

½ oz Manuka honey mix

½ oz mixed berry puree or muddled berries

2 oz Barr Hill Barrel Aged Old Tom Gin

½ oz Nux Alpina or Nocino

1 oz fresh lemon juice

1-2 oz Bundaberg Ginger Beer

Shake all but the ginger beer with ice. Strain over fresh ice in a Collins glass. Top with ginger beer. Garnish with skewered blueberry and raspberry.

The Groveyard Shift

Specific strains of honey really get more recognized for certain types of baking. Orange blossom honey, for instance, gets renown for its bright flavor in baklava. It gets its citrusy aroma and flavor from the orange blossoms in orange groves. Therefore this honey typically reigns in Florida and California.

Hello Sunshine

½ oz orange blossom honey mix

½ oz date syrup

¾ oz Amaro Montenegro

1.5 oz Cazadores or Altos Anejo Tequila

1 oz muddled pineapple juice

½ oz lemon juice

Place a few pineapple chunks into a shaker and press out the juice using a muddler. Add all other ingredients with ice and shake the mixture. Strain over new ice in a Collins glass. Garnish a dried date and orange peel on a skewer.

That's the Rub

I struggle with the savory drink category. I admit it's one of my greatest weaknesses as a mixer. I shy away from fat-washing spirits, root vegetable juices, and all that. Leave the meat and veggies for your plate after the aperitif. I'll mess about with tamarind and all manner of spices, earthy plant spirits like Cynar . . . but trying to generate a truly genius savory cocktail does my fucking head in.

So salted honey kind of takes away the rub (or does it add the rub?). Writer's block is setting in at this point. I'll take this combination of salted honey, wheaty whiskey, and sweet caraway as a small victory. Hell, each bit of this book is another baby step.

Old Salt

1 oz salted honey mix

¾ oz fresh lime juice

1.5 oz Weller Special Reserve Bourbon
   (or good affordable wheat whiskey)

¾ oz Combier Kummel

1 dash Angostura aromatic bitters

2 dashes mole or cocoa bitters

Shake all ingredients with ice and strain over fresh ice in a rocks glass. Express a lemon peel over the drink surface and add it as a garnish.

A Vulgaris Display

Most strains of honey gain their unique character from plant pollen specific to a geographic area. Heather honey gets its sophisticated blend of aromas and flavors from heather flowers (Calluna Vulgaris) in Scotland. Subtle hints of bitter, tangy, and smoky notes come across in the flavor. Your nose will pick up warm, woody fruit aromas. Sort of faint, ghostly hints of things other than just honey.

In that spirit, this cocktail takes inspiration from an early 20th century ghost story at Scotland's Broomhill Castle. The story goes that adventurer Captain McNeil fell in love with Sita, an Indian princess, and brought her home to live in the castle. She struggled to adjust to the new surroundings and soon began to embarrass and irritate the captain, who locked her away in the castle. Her mysterious disappearance led to sightings of a castle ghost who later became known as the "Black Lady".

Heather honey joins hands with Scottish spirits and native tree fruits such as plum, cherry and pear. The cardamom bitters leave an eerie hint of Indian spice.

The Black Lady of Broomhill

½ oz Scottish heather honey mix

1 oz dark tart cherry juice

1 oz Speyburn 10 Single Malt Scotch

1 oz Rothman & Winter Pear cordial

2 dashes Fee Brothers Plum Bitters

2 dashes cardamom bitters

Shake all ingredients with ice and strain over new ice cubes in a Collins glass. Garnish with a skewered dark cherry.

Black Lady of Broomhill (left),
Old Salt

Mead You Look

Mead resembles beer in the way it's made, but it's primarily made with honey and normally still rather than bubbly. It's made some progress into cocktail mixing, usually at meaderies.
I do quite enjoy it despite its association with medieval times. The only way you'd get me into a renaissance fair is heavily armed and whooped up on PCP.

Vikings favored mead, however, drinking it from hollow animal horns between torture sessions called "blood eagles". Look it up. If that doesn't appeal to your dark side, I simply can't imagine what will. If they did those at renaissance fairs, I'd probably go to them on the regular.

In my experience, meads often taste of muscat grapes with a tendency towards honeyish sweetness rather than dryness. Those flavors guided me towards the drink you see here.

Heathen Chemistry

1 oz traditional or cherry mead (non-carbonated)

1.5 oz Smith & Cross Navy Rum

½ oz Cruzan Blackstrap Rum

½ oz ginger syrup

½ oz fresh lemon juice

Shake all ingredients with ice and serve over fresh ice in a small laboratory beaker. Add dry ice for effect. Garnish with mint and lime.

Baren Wasteland

Getting lumped in with an infantry of vile honey spirits, I think Barenjager takes a bit of a bad rap. It's honestly about the only honey spirit I'd use to modify and sweeten a cocktail. Everyone else gets in bed with Drambuie, which triggers my gag reflex just thinking about it. Perhaps it's a misguided association with Jagermeister, another misunderstood German spirit. Jager can be enjoyed like any other classic amaro, but somehow instead got marketed to frat bars as a brain eraser.

Most mixtures using Barenjager lean sweet because the spirit is intensely sweet. This little number is no exception. Think of it as a campfire drink for the Black Forest in winter.

Blood Trail from the Bear Trap

1 oz Barenjager

½ oz Cherry Heering

1 oz Punt e Mes vermouth

½ oz Genepy des Alpes

2 dashes King Floyd's Scorched Pear & Ginger Bitters

Add all liquids with ice into a mixing glass and top with ice. Stir mixture until chilled and strain over a large format ice cube in a rocks glass.

Blood Trail from the Bear Trap (left),
Heathen Chemistry

Chapter 4: Breakfast at Timothy's
(a.k.a. Leggo my Drinko)

I already kind of regret the title of this chapter. It's catchy, yeah. But I hate the formal spelling of my first name. It reminds me that my parents took it from a chapter of the bible. And as it turns out, that's probably my least favorite work of fiction.

Challenge me. It's technically fiction. Prove me wrong.

Anyhow, I've never kept it a secret that I normally let others do the heavy lifting when it comes to syrups. Sure, it's cool to make your own orgeat and tell all your friends that you made it. But then you get to clean up the boiled almond goo from your kitchen. I'd rather have six different expressions of orgeat from those that earn their living and reputations making it.

In my explorations for syrups, I discovered that some small producers make exotic flavors like saskatoon, elderberry, mulberry . . . the list goes on and on. These producers clearly aimed at a pancake-consuming market, not mixologists. In fact, companies like Runamok create some insanely good twists on classic maple syrup. But as long as the syrups were thin enough or mixed with water, they made some pretty tasty adult beverages very much possible.

This chapter celebrates the vast array of syrups that don't normally spring to mind when you think of cocktails. I hate to adopt that stupid novelty t-shirt phrase attributed to beer, but in truth, syrup does not strictly have to be for breakfast anymore. We'll stroll through a few lesser-known but more cocktail-focused syrups too.

Since we're mucking about with a lot of syrups technically intended for pancakes, we may as well throw in some coffee cocktails. Day drinking does, after all, require some constitution.

Don't Let the Label Scare You . . .

Lyle's in England produces both a golden syrup and a much darker counterpart, black treacle. This pales by comparison to the dark macabre nature of the illustration on a bottle or tin of either sryup. Look closely and you'll see that, indeed, it depicts a dead lion covered in bees. Mind you this tradition hails from its origin in 1881.

Abram Lyle drew inspiration for this odd art from the biblical tale of Samson, who bare-handedly killed a lion. Seems enough of a dick move, yeah? But no, Samson returns to the lion's rotting carcass days later to, I don't know, get a selfie for Instagram? He finds that bees built a hive in the lion's dead body. So he extracts honey from the bees' new furry condo, then gives it to his parents without telling them where he got it.

The bible better indeed be fiction, because weird "heroic" assholes like this give believers their role models. But once again, I digress.

Weirdness aside, Lyle's makes very interesting syrups that are really more aimed at baking, breakfasts, and desserts. But fuck me if I'm not going to put them in some drinks. I hope you like these. One is made with their golden syrup and bears a similar color, while the black treacle concoction is, well . . . black.

Gold Lion

- ¾ oz Lyle's Golden Syrup mix
- ½ oz Fratello Hazelnut spirit
- ½ oz St George NOLA Coffee Liqueur
- 1 oz Angostura 5 Year Rum
- 1.5 oz Granny Smith apple juice
- 2 dashes Angostura aromatic bitters

Black Adam

- 0.5 oz Lyle's Black Treacle
- 1 oz Glenmorangie X Whisky
- 0.5 teaspoon activated charcoal (optional—only adds color and no flavor)
- 1.5 oz pear nectar
- 0.5 Patron Citronge Orange
- 0.5 oz Amaro di Angostura

Shake all ingredients with ice and strain mixture over a large cube in a rocks glass. Lay a dried cinnamon apple slice on top of the cube.

Pandan, Thank You, Ma'am

Pandan is often called fragrant screwpine or vanilla grass in English. Its grassy vanilla flavor gives a unique southeast Asian earthiness to an otherwise plain simple syrup. Natural Pandan extract can be found online, just like other interesting Asian extracts like ube. Only a few drops transform simple syrup into a tasty green elixir.

Don't take my word for it. The extract comes in tiny bottles, but a single inexpensive vessel will make a lasting supply of Pandan simple syrup. Try it in this whimsical interpretation of a gin fizz. Then try creating something else with it.

Turn of the Screwpine

¾ oz Pandan simple syrup

2 oz Tanqueray 10 Gin

½ oz Patron Citronge Mango cordial

¾ oz fresh lime juice

2 dashes Bar Keep apple bitters

1 egg white or 1 spoon aquafaba

1-2 oz club soda

Shake all ingredients with ice and strain over new ice in a tall Collins or zombie glass. Top with club soda. Garnish with mango cubes on a bamboo skewer.

Hamburg Hayride

Woodruff syrup might prove a bit elusive to find, but it's well worth the quest because it has such a unique and distinct flavor. You'll see that it also has an equally distinct intense green color. It tastes sweet and earthy, almost hay-like. Traditionally, Germans add this syrup to Berliner Weisse beer to cut the acidity of this dry beer style.

In its native Germany, the locals call the woodruff plant "waldmeister" or "master of the woods". The traditional Waldmeister version has a radiant green color, though you may find more pale or straw-colored woodruff as well. The cocktail that follows takes its influence from the traditional beer mixtures made in its homeland

Wood Nymph

1 oz woodruff syrup

1.5 oz Woodford Reserve Straight Malt Whiskey

¾ oz fresh lemon juice

½ oz Pierre Ferrand or Giffard Framboise cordial

Shake all ingredients with ice and strain over fresh ice in a rocks glass. Garnish with a fresh raspberry.

Turn of the Screwpine (left),
Wood Nymph

Kick out the Yams

Sometimes an artisan syrup producer comes along with an unexpectedly unique sweetener—one so singular that you just order it immediately, knowing you'll come up with the cocktail later. El Guapo makes these types of syrups, as well as several never-duplicated bitters. So when I discovered their new sweet potato syrup, it was on order within minutes.

Producers like this make my job easy, well . . . easier. I've always said it's great to lean on others for the heavy lifting when it comes to the messy, time-consuming things that would hold your kitchen hostage, while summarily eating into your drinking time. Syrups don't really offend me until they take ALL the thought and work out of drink creativity—things like "Old Fashioned" syrups. If you're too lazy to muddle sugar and bitters, you shouldn't be reading this book.

Digging for Fire

¾ oz El Guapo Sweet Potato syrup

¼ oz Pasubio Vino Amaro

½ oz Barrow's Intense Ginger spirit

1.5 oz Sagamore Spirit Cask Strength Rye

1 oz key lime juice

2 dashes Bittermen's Xocolatl Mole Bitters

Shake all ingredients with ice and strain over fresh ice in a tulip glass. Garnish with candied ginger and lime peel on a skewer.

In The Thick of It

Molasses—the thick, dark goo left over from sugar refining. It's also the stuff of life for most rums. Some companies also make fruit blend molasses that in turn make great cocktail sweeteners. Look for pomegranate molasses, for example, from producers like Cortas while shopping for orange blossom and rose waters at Middle Eastern markets.

More recently, BG Reynolds began producing pineapple molasses using the recipe from Devil's Reef. It can't be understated how happy it makes me when a unique bartender's invention is shared with others. It gains visibility for the bar, the inventing bartender, and the craft producer that abides by its creator's recipe. It also makes it much easier for lazy twats like me to invent new drinks.

Mosquito Coast

1 oz Clement VSOP Rum

¾ oz BG Reynolds Pineapple Molasses

½ oz St George Raspberry Brandy
(or framboise cordial)

1 oz fresh squeezed orange juice

½ oz Cruzan Blackstrap Rum

Shake all ingredients with ice and strain over fresh ice in a large rocks or Mai Tai glass. Skewer an orange peel and pineapple cube as a garnish.

Mosquito Coast (left),
Digging for Fire

Old Fassioned

As of the penning of this tome, the cocktail world is busy resurrecting fassionola syrup from a mysterious past. Another author, in fact, should be releasing a book fully devoted to the topic of fassionola about the same time this book hits the shelves.

To sum up, a German chemist invented Passiflora, a passion fruit syrup for ice cream and sodas in the early 20th century. Thereafter it made its way into cocktails as Fassionola, then virtually disappeared from sight for quite some time. Only recently have craft syrup-makers given it new life.

Fassionola typically blends passion fruit with other types of tropical fruit, hence its more beloved presence in tiki cocktails such as heritage recipe Hurricanes. The syrup also typically shared its vibrant red color with the drinks in which it was used.

Rather than drift into the predictable tropical genre that earns my keep, I mixed fassionola with the most oddball flavors with which it can be paired.

Someday Sweetheart

¾ oz red fassionola syrup

1 oz wheated bourbon

½ oz kummel or Danish style aquavit

¼ oz allspice or pimento dram

1 oz strawberry nectar

Shake all ingredients with ice and serve over ice in a pilsner glass. Garnish with a strawberry and star anise on a bamboo skewer.

Autocracy

Autocrat brand coffee syrup hails from Rhode Island. Natives of the state blend this intense java syrup with milk to make "coffee milk". I love this syrup for its unique and unmistakable flavor. This drink pays tribute to the local dairy concoction that made it famous, but includes some fun flavor companions for strong coffee.

Hail Caesar

½ oz Autocrat Coffee Syrup

½ oz Mathilde Cassis cordial

1 oz Martell VS Cognac

1 oz Banks 5 or Tiki Lovers White Rum

½ oz half & half

2 dashes cocoa or mole bitters

Stir all ingredients with ice and serve over a large ice cube in a rocks glass. Lay a few blueberries on top of the cube.

Someday Sweetheart (left),
Hail Caesar

Chapter 5: Kick out the Jams
Shaking with Jams, Jellies and Fruit-Infused Gins

"I hope Wayne Kramer can forgive me for using an MC5 song title to celebrate jams and jellies." I hope he's is more flattered than litigant.

Buffalo, New York bears many similarities to my home city of Cleveland, Ohio. Like home, it faced decades of "mistake on Lake Erie" jokes. Derelict property nearly dwarfed the liveable structures. Pierogies were considered a food group. These sad parallels cursed our respective lakeside zip codes for far too long.

Much like Cleveland, Buffalo had nowhere to go but up. While our city ramped up its culinary and cocktail game, so did Buffalo. We visited Buffalo about 25 years ago, while still mired in its sad period. It lasted about 4 hours before we fled into Canada for the slightly more cultured experience that only Niagara Falls could offer.

Cast your mind forward to just a couple years ago, when we visited a completely different Buffalo. We stayed with a couple friends that know the city well, and know their way around a cocktail even more. They took us on a whirlwind weekend through the city's new, independent gems: Buffalo Proper, Hydraulic Hearth, and a blur of many other hotspots.

Among these, Ballyhoo stands out the most in my memory. It stood alone atop a small, cinder block structure amidst acres of parking lot between General Mills and the local casino. It was kind of a secret hideout for the cocktail-wary and local bar industry people alike. The place hosted an astounding back bar and drink menu with very little spare space. More to the point, they created a genius concept called "jam sessions".

Jam sessions helped make Ballyhoo an even greater hideaway to visit. Guests could choose from an array of several different craft jams and jellies from England. This was then paired with the base spirit of your choice. The bar staff would blend this pairing with any juices, bitters or other elements to form a perfect cocktail, all on the fly.

This chapter carries on that inspiration. It really kind of segues from the concept of the previous chapter on syrups. Even though many unusual syrups are out there waiting to be discovered, they don't complete the landscape of sweet flavor options. Jams very much fill those gaps. They simply have a different texture and behavior to consider when you mix with them.

Much to my pleasure, some gin distillers have begun making gins infused with fruits traditionally reserved for jams and pie fillings. These sweeter gin hybrids pony up some great flavors with which to experiment. More thoughtful and carefully made than flavored vodkas, infused gins will not flood the market. I feature some of my favorites at the end of this chapter.

Tart of Darkness

English distiller Whitney Neill makes one of the more interesting ranges of exotically flavored gins. Among such expressions as blood orange, rhubarb and ginger, and raspberry, WN also makes a quince gin. Apparently this tart, golden pome fruit lends itself well to making spirits. It's not just for poncey English jams.

To balance out the tart side of the quince, I did a rare thing and blended two gins in this cocktail. The other is the sweeter berry expression of Bombay Sapphire Bramble. The remaining parts draw entirely from fruits. I feel this blend actually draws elements from all four seasons, so enjoy it year-round.

Quinc(e)y Jones

1 oz Whitley Neill Quince Gin

1 oz Bombay Sapphire Bramble Gin

1 oz 100% pomegranate juice

½ oz fresh lemon juice

¾ oz passion fruit syrup

Shake all ingredients with ice and serve over ice in a pilsner glass. Garnish with fresh raspberries on a cocktail skewer.

Tom, Dick and Sherry

The accidental discovery of olallieberry jam inspired me towards this drink. The weird odyssey of this berry begins with a couple of mad berry breeders who crossed black loganberries with youngberries. And this excludes the hybridized berries that spawned those berries. But it comes from Oregon. And those fuckers known berries. Have a marionberry sometime. Then you'll know it's not an opinion, it's a fact.

The absence of olallieberry jam from your cupboard does not prevent you from making a tasty beverage. It resembles raspberries, blackberries, and the like. So you can simply obtain a good jar of craft mixed berry jam. The blend of berry flavors works quite famously with citrus and all of the rich, razzle-dazzle spirits outlined below.

Tom-Tom Club

1 oz Barr Hill Barrel-Aged Old Tom Gin

1 oz Tom's Foolery Applejack (or sub Laird's)

1 heaping bar spoon olallieberry jam
  (or mixed berry jam)

½ oz Sandeman Armada Cream Sherry

½ oz fresh Meyer lemon juice

2 dashes Angostura Bitters

Shake all but bitters with ice and serve over ice in a tall Collins glass. Dash bitters over the drink surface. Garnish with skewered berries.

TomTom Club (left),
Quinc(e)y Jones

The Kiwi Takes Flight

Kiwi fruit gets kind of a shit rap, I think. It too often appears in some lackluster kiwi-strawberry soft drink and that's all people know of it. While that's a very natural flavor pairing, this fruit offers much more breadth than its flightless bird's namesake.

Following a lengthy sidewinding through the myriad of kiwi's best bedfellows, I arrived at this mixture. It struck me that it incorporates red, gold and green components. While I'm not so much a fan of Culture Club, many culturally rich nations adopted these colors into their flag. I chose Congo as a sideways tribute to Congo Powers, legendary member of The Cramps, Gun Club, and his own Pink Monkey Birds.

Congo Powers

1 heaping bar spoon of kiwi jam or puree

1 heaping bar spoon red currant jam

1.5 oz Bounty or Wray & Nephew Gold Rum

½ oz apple brandy

½ oz bianco vermouth

1 oz fresh lemon OR lime juice

2 dashes Bittermen's Krupnik Honey Bitters

Shake all ingredients with ice and strain over pebble ice in a tulip glass or snifter. Garnish with mint, lemon and edible flower.

Quincing the Night Away

Quince is weird. As a hard, tart fruit, it defies being eaten right from the tree. It has to be cooked, then turned into a jam, jelly or marmalade, or infused into a spirit. But it's a nice golden aromatic fruit that begs for attention in drink form. Belly up to this spicy winter concoction. Quince might just be your jam.

Fool's Gold

1 heaping bar spoon quince jam or jelly

½ oz Royal Rose Cardamom Clove Syrup

1 oz unfiltered honeycrisp apple juice

1.5 oz Cazadores Anejo Tequila

¾ oz Marsala wine

2 drops rose water

Shake all ingredients with ice and strain mixture over fresh ice in a snifter. Garnish with an orange wedge punctured with dried, whole cloves.

Congo Powers (left),
Fool's Gold

More Adventures with Toast Spreads

My previous book included a bourbon cocktail made with apple butter called Teddy Roosevelt's Fox. It turned out splendidly. I dropped this one on every whiskey event menu I did. Many of them were consumed at said events, fulfilling my constant need for morsels of validation.

Then I discovered pear butter. Gosh, I hope plum butter exists, just in case I have a third book in me.

The apple butter cocktail was a polygamy of natural winter flavors. It betrothed walnut bitters, sherry, and honey with a very warming whiskey. So the pear butter drink had to be a great, weird B-side to the original A-side. Otherwise anyone reading this after buying the first book would just accuse me of plagiarizing myself.

So here it is—a tropical-inspired drink, made with a homespun toast spread that old people eat.

Partridge in a Palm Tree

1 heaping spoon of pear butter

½ oz passion fruit spirit (Passoa or Giffard Fruit de la Passion)

1.5 oz Pussers Gunpowder Rum

¼ oz Bitter Truth EXR

½ oz cinnamon syrup

¾ oz fresh lemon juice

1 dash mole or chocolate bitters

Shake all ingredients with ice. Strain over fresh ice in a snifter. Garnish with coffee beans on the drinks surface.

When Life Gives You Lemons, Drink.

You haven't lived if deprived of the tart, creamy wonder of lemon curd. To this day it bedazzles cakes, pastries and toasted breads across the English countryside.

It took me way too long to consider lemon curd in a cocktail. It gives you sweet and citrus in one go, along with the silky texture of egg white. I hope no one else ever thought of this because I feel like a fucking genius at this moment.

Perhaps more interesting is how this unfolded into a pretty weird stepchild of a Fog Cutter.

Earl of Lemongrab

1 heaping bar spoon lemon curd or lemon marmalade

1.5 oz Boodles Mulberry Gin

½ oz aged brandy

½ oz Oloroso or other rich sherry

1 oz unfiltered apple juice or orchard cider

2 dashes peach bitters

Shake all ingredients with ice and strain over a large format ice cube in a rocks glass.

Earl of Lemongrab (left),
Partridge in a Palm Tree

Nothing to do with Wolverine

I don't want you to think of the Marvel character Logan when reading this bit. This section doffs my hat to the unique Loganberry that hails from Britain, like so many other good things. Such as Captain Britain. More specifically Alan Moore's Captain Britain, and really just the second half of his run.

This being my book and hence my soapbox, I must say those Wolverine movies get vastly over-praised. That last Logan film made everyone go "oh man, it's so dark and gritty!". Meanwhile it ends with a mouseketeer troupe of goofy kids running through the woods with him. And what the fuck was Stephen Merchant supposed to be? An underfed albino alien butler?

Okay, back to loganberries. These stand apart from similar fruits like raspberry and blackberry. Their intense wine-red color rivals the intensity of their tart flavor. This pairs nicely with conversely sweet and dark fruit flavors, and particularly dark fortified wine. You'll likely need to seek out an English brand of loganberry jam, but it will pay off both in this drink and on your morning crumpet.

Heering Aid

1 heaping bar spoon loganberry jam

¼ oz Riga Black Balsam spirit

1 oz Cherry Heering

½ oz Rothman & Winter Apricot cordial

1.5 oz Fuji apple juice

Ruby port float

Shake all liquids with ice and strain over ice in a Collins glass. Float a small layer of red port on top. Garnish with three dark brandied cherries on a cocktail pick.

Chapter 6: Hot Mess
The Joys of Spicy and Smoky Mixing

Tequila's renaissance and burgeoning array of new cocktails have ushered in some spicy heat along with them. Warming peppery spirits like Ancho Reyes and Ancho Reyes Verde have made this easier on people in the profession. Lest we overlook the jalapeno infusions and fiery salts that have ramped up the spicy margarita game.

The heatwave, by no means, ends with a margarita flight, however.

The spice burn can accent a number of spirits like whiskey and rum, too. And trust me, I don't abide Jack Fire, Fireball, or other such nonsense. One can create a better, more balanced cocktail by applying their own fire. Correctly applied spices also play well off of tropical fruits and a vast array of syrups.

You can add a spicy bite to any cocktail using hotter blends of craft bitters, or by doing your own simple spirit or syrup infusions with peppers or other warm spices. It takes little effort and gives you a few more bragging rights when it comes to showcasing your creativity.

Spicing drinks will usually appeal to anyone that leans towards savory flavors. This can also help temper the sugary side of otherwise overly sweet drinks. Likewise, smoke has become an increasingly popular means to adjust the aroma and flavors of typically sweeter and more spirit-forward drinks like Manhattans and Old Fashioneds.

You can use a smoker device (as described in Chapter 1) to float a layer of smoke over the surface of a cocktail. This coats the liquid and glass surfaces, thereby giving your drink a more natural smoke aroma. Many different types of wood chips like applewood, oak, and hickory offer you different aroma accents on fall and winter drinks.

Just be warned. When you smoke one or more cocktails, everyone gets so bedazzled that you'll likely get stuck making them all night. I mean, all you're doing is trapping smoke in a bell jar. What the hell? It's not like I'm conjuring an evil spirit from a crack in the earth . . . .

Or am I? . . .

Other less laborious or occult-driven means of imparting smoky flavors are there for you too. You can buy bitters and syrups that the crafter has smoked. Smoky spirits like Mezcal and certain types of Scotch give you the inflection of natural smoke without all the hoodoo.

Ok, so what if I'm also drenching myself in freshly-spilled chicken blood when I smoke cocktails. Perhaps also dancing nude in a pentagram. Don't judge.

Ilegal Substances

Ilegal (or "Illegal") mezcals hold a special place for me considering my ongoing servitude to the state of Ohio. I believe it's the only brand sold here offering silver (unaged), reposado (barrel rested), and anejo (barrel aged) expressions. Further to that, it's not astronomically expensive for seriously good mezcal.

So cue up some songs about standoffs with the Federales. This drink goes heavy on the mezcal, putting you in the mind of a smoking gun. If it's difficult finding piloncillo, you can make this with simple syrup made from unrefined brown sugar syrup.

Sandinista

1 oz Ilegal Reposado Mezcal

1 oz Bounty Gold Rum

½ oz Noble Cut Limecello or Patron Citronge Lime cordial

¾ oz fresh tangerine juice

½ oz Piloncillo (Mexican brown sugar) syrup

Sal de Gusano Agave Worm Salt Rim

Swirl the pulp of a lemon wedge around a rocks glass rim. Dip the rim in piloncillo. Shake all liquid ingredients and strain over fresh ice in the glass. Garnish with lime.

Crazy from the Heat

This is the only drink containing vodka in this book. Period. I do this cautiously. It comes off quite hypocritical, considering my multiple rants against this typically bland spirit. Outside of the flavor infusions I'd make with this otherwise pointless spirit, St George Green Chile Vodka is the only vodka I'll keep in my house.

Considering the complexity of producing St George's GCV, I find it difficult to actually call this spirit vodka. The base spirit is distilled with several fresh California peppers, cilantro, and lime peels, creating a potently hot and vegetal spirit that has a lovely natural straw color. So in the end, it pretty well rejects the colorless, odorless and flavorless spirit after which it's named.

St George Green Chile Vodka surely adds a kick to a morning recovery bloody mary. Because of its intense heat and flavor, I leaned on Karen Page's Flavor Bible to come up with a recipe that balances the cocktail. I hope that you'll find this Mexico-inspired/ borderline tiki concoction does just that.

Summer's Cauldron

½ oz St George Green Chile Vodka

½ oz Giffard Banane du Bresil

½ oz Giffard Crème de Cacao

1.5 oz fresh pineapple juice

½ oz cinnamon syrup

2 dashes Bittercube Blackstrap Bitters

Shake all ingredients with ice and strain over fresh ice in a Pilsner glass. Dress up with a swizzle and fancy straw.

Summer's Cauldron (left),
Sandinista

Forest Fires

Smokey the Bear would likely disapprove of this section title. But when I started playing with smoked maple syrup, my mind drifted straight into piney flavors and charred wood. As many tasteless arson jokes as I make, I'd never burn a forest. I only used the woods to hide adult magazines as a youngster. So there's really no motivation.

There's quite a nice subtle smoke aroma and flavor in this cocktail. But if you really want some forest fire, go ahead and add a layer of real smoke over the ice using a smoker.

Arson Garden

½ oz Tipplemen's Smoked Maple Syrup

1.5 oz barrel-aged Bols Genever gin

¾ oz Carpano Classico red vermouth

½ oz Amaro Montenegro

2 dashes Pink House Alchemy Smoldered Bitters

Stir all ingredients with ice and strain over a large ice cube in a rocks glass. Garnish with a smoked rosemary sprig.

Optional: add a layer of smoke using your smoker.

Cumin to America

It takes weird little cues to nudge me toward savory cocktails. Case in point—a cumin spice aimed at cocktails. Perhaps in part due to my tiki background, I've found that exotic cooking spices like this are good bedfellows with tropical flavors. Behold this odd creation and see if you agree.

Minnesota Masala

1-2 dashes of Addition Cumin Cocktail Spice

1 oz aged or clear aquavit

1 oz Diplomatico Planas Rum

½ oz Giffard Coconut syrup

¾ oz fresh lime juice

Tajin or red chile spice for rim

Moisten the rim of a rocks or Mai Tai glass with lime juice. Dip the rim in Tajin or red chile spice. Shake all the drink ingredients with ice and serve over ice in the rimmed glass. Place a lime wedge on the edge of the glass.

Arson Garden (left),
Minnesota Masala

Carpe Capiscum

Admittedly "hot stuff" falls outside my comfort zone. I've never understood why nuclear-powered hot sauces became such a craze. What would draw anyone towards a bottle of sauce sporting a fat bumpkin screaming in agony? I've also learned the hard way what happens when you crack a Chinese chile pod.

That being said, chili syrups and spirits work a treat when blended into a balanced cocktail. Spicy warmth compliments spirits like tequila and rum quite well. Take for example this whimsically tropical creation.

Chengdu Hustle

¼ oz Fly By Jing Sovereign Syrup

1.5 oz papaya juice

½ oz Mathilde Peche cordial

1 oz Japanese plum wine

1 oz reposado tequila

1 oz pure pomegranate juice

Shake all ingredients with ice and serve on ice in a tulip glass or snifter. Garnish with a dried chile.

The Devil Made Me Do It

The classic daiquiri probably gives you the perfect foundation for unlimited riffs. Just start with the basics—simple syrup, lime juice and any type of rum—and you can build some pretty stellar creations. Play with flavors, strength, and modifiers and more often than not, you'll have guests thinking you're a goddamn genius.

In that stead, I give you the Devil's Daiquiri. I wanted this to hit you with hints of heat and spice with a slyly boozy backbone. Enjoy too many, however, and damnation awaits the next day.

Hold that thought. The NEXT drink will knock you down to Tartarus, which is like the hell of hell.

The Devil's Daiquiri

1 oz Angostura White Oak Rum

1 oz Plantation OFTD Rum

½ oz Ancho Reyes

¾ oz fresh lime juice

¾ oz Demerara simple syrup

2 dashes Bittermen's Hellfire Shrub Bitters

Combine all ingredients in a shaker with ice. Shake until chilled and strain mixture into a chilled coupe glass. Float a thin wheel of lime on the drink surface.

Señor Peligro (left),
The Devil's Daiquiri

Rio Grande Bloodbath

The Devil's Daiquiri might be more of a practice cocktail for this one.

This drink takes me back to a time when I favored craft beer, particularly Stone Brewing creations. From the outset, Stone was all about breaking molds but maintaining good flavor balance in each brew. And then sometimes, they just wanted to fuck with you.

Among their litany of perfected India pales and roasty stouts stood two merciless beers, one called Crime and the other Punishment. These potently boozy brews were made with brutal amounts of west coast ghost peppers. I could scarcely consume a thimble of either without wrestling back tears. They backhanded you across the face and then laughed "I bet you're glad you spent $20 a bottle, you ludicrous little worm".

Stone's overall philosophy, whether unconsciously or not, seems to fit my operator's manual for cocktailing: really think about flavors and balance, but sometimes inflict suffering on those guests you really want to rue waking up tomorrow. The drink featured here definitely falls into the latter category. It came to me when listening to Ministry, fueling an already furious mood. And I just wanted to hurt people. Badly.

So here it is: a cocktail that's made with really good craft ingredients, but sets you up for bar-brawling with broken bottles. And only your cuts, bruises and scorched palette will remind you what happened the night before.

Señor Peligro

2 oz Hampden Estate Overproof

¾ oz Ancho Reyes Verde

¼ oz Del Maguey Vida Mezcal

½ oz Bees Knees Spicy Honey

¾ oz key lime juice

½ oz Giffard coconut syrup

3 dashes Infuse Tres Amigos Bitters

Shake all ingredients with ice and strain over pebble ice in a Mai Tai glass. Garnish with lime and fresh cut jalapeño peppers.

Basquerade Party

Spicy pepper spirits can come off a bit hokey, just like the avalanche of hot sauces that dare people to corrode their digestive tracts. But the market bears some real gems like Ancho Reyes that offer your drink creations a great pepper backbone without cueing the waterworks.

Giffard's Piment d'Espelette might just eclipse all the other pepper spirits I've tasted. Giffard macerates peppers from the French commune of Espelette, historically the northern home of the Basques, in rhum agricole. It combines the flavor of peppers native only to this obscure region of France with the earthy funk of Martinique rum. You struggle to find something as uniquely aromatic, warm and spicy as this spirit.

Anyone who reads my rants knows my undying devotion to the Giffard line of spirits. It gives me a glimmer of hope that my home state of Ohio won't damn residents with mixing aspirations only to flavored vodkas. Enjoy another love letter to Giffard.

Andresito the Ghost

- ¾ oz Giffard Piment d'Espelette
- ¾ oz Genepy des Alpes
- ¾ oz Martell Cognac
- ¾ oz fresh lime juice
- ½ oz Demerara simple syrup
- 2 dashes Boker's Bitters (or cardamom bitters from another producer)

Shake all ingredients with ice and strain into a chilled coupe. Garnish with a lime wheel.

Hellfire in the Pacific

Thank goodness for the people at National Geographic. They educate and entertain you. And for people like me, they also inspire cocktails.

Kilauea in Hawaii remains the world's most active volcano. It's been belching up lava for 30 years and counting. I find it metaphorical for my unending hubris and foul temper. And it also planted the idea in my mind for perhaps the world's first stirred tiki cocktail. Meh, someone else probably did it, but fuck me if I'm going to do that extra research. Tell my publisher if you discover otherwise.

Remember that smoker I suggested in Chapter 1? Here's another chance to use it. It will give a nice smoky aroma and steaming volcanic visual zing to this drink. Think of this as basically a tiki-esque old fashioned. It brings together classic tiki spirits but subtracts the juices that would typically make it a shaken drink.

This recipe specifies Appleton 15, which can usually bring bourbon fiends over to the rum camp. But other reputable Caribbean rums with a high age statement will work.

Kilauea

- 1.5 oz Appleton 15 Year Rum
- ½ oz cold brew concentrate
- ¼ oz Bitter Truth Pimento Dram
- ½ oz Copper & Kings Destillaire Intense Orange Curacao (or sub Ferrand)
- ½ oz demerara sugar or syrup
- 2 dashes Angostura Cocoa Bitters
- 1 pomelo or grapefruit peel and Kona coffee bean

Place the peel in a mixing glass and drench it with the sugar/syrup and bitters. Muddle the peel into the liquids. Add the spirits and ice. Stir until the ice level drops and the mix is adequately diluted. Strain the mix over a large ice cube in a Mai Tai glass. Add the peel to the glass and lay the coffee bean on top of the ice cube.

Optional: Using your smoker, apply a layer of applewood chip smoke over the drink surface.

Chapter 7: Juiced Up
The Joys of Exotic Nectars

This chapter owes its existence to happy accidents. Particularly those that happen when you find oddball fruits and juices you never expected. This magic moment has given me more creative fodder than any other real acumen in the spirits world.

This lightning obviously strikes a lot harder when you visit specialty cocktail shops like Cocktail Emporium in Toronto, where you can find exotic juices like Sudachi and Yuzu. More often, I'd happen upon strange juices and fruits like elderberry, gooseberry, and blood orange just strolling through import and specialty food markets.

In my mind, these happenings portend the creation of cocktails.

This chapter gives you several shaken delights that lean heavily upon juices for their unique flavors. Some call for fresh juices that appear seasonally, while others can be made year-round. I'd encourage you to keep a keen eye open even on everyday grocery trips. You never know what inspiration awaits when you constantly think in terms of cocktailing.

Even simple twists on garden variety juices can give new dimensions to your drinks. Try using Meyer lemon or key lime instead of your standard issue citrus. Hell, even fresh cranberry juice can be put to positive use. It's not just for the infuriating entitled housewives that make you coach them through a cocktail decision for ten minutes, only to arrive at a vodka & cran.

That really happens. It makes you question your career decisions. Honestly, it lulls you into a fantasy realm where you soak these guests in Wray & Nephew overproof and set fire to them. Over, and over, and over. As much as that would be a waste of good overproof.

I hope you enjoy this chapter as much as I enjoy fantasizing about white-privilege vodka & cran drinkers engulfed in flames. Screaming. In slow motion.

Fruits and Vegetables

Fresh-squeezed watermelon juice makes for insanely good cocktails, especially during summer. It also makes an insufferable mess. You have to cut it up, run it through a blender, then mesh strain it into a container.

Even a mini melon yields quite a lot of juice. And watermelon mingles really well with peppers and other vegetable flavors. This drink mixes up some traditional flavors of the Caribbean and Mexico, so it's perfect for hotter climes. If poblano peppers' vegetal flavor isn't your jam, swap out the pepper spirit to something you like better.

I named this drink after the Spanish word for "dragonfly". I have no idea why.

Libuela

2 oz Chairman's Reserve Silver Rum

1.5 oz fresh watermelon juice

½ oz panela simple syrup (or sub raw brown sugar syrup)

¼-½ oz Ancho Reyes Verde

2-3 fresh cut jalapeno pepper rings

Shake all liquid ingredients with ice and strain over a large format ice cube in a large rocks or Mai Tai glass. Lay pepper rings on the surface of the cube.

Blood Feud

The seasonal window for blood oranges frustrates me endlessly. For some reason it seems like a matter of minutes. Then the rest of the year deprives you of its vibrantly deep crimson purple and flavorful juice. Its rind and pulp also make for a more dazzling garnish than its year-round cousins in the citrus world.

So during its fleeting appearances between October and May, make this drink. You can even find bottled non-concentrate, natural blood orange juice if you look hard enough. Perhaps the more elusive part of this beverage will be the kumquat syrup. It's a natural pairing with the blood orange. But more likely, you will have to find dried kumquats online and simmer them in simple syrup. Trust me. It will all be worth it.

Crimson Countess

1 oz blood orange juice

½ oz kumquat simple syrup

¼ oz cinnamon syrup

¼ oz Bitter Truth EXR (or Amaro di Angostura)

1 oz Banks 5 Rum

1 oz Cazadores Anejo Tequila

Shake all ingredients with ice and strain over fresh ice in a hurricane glass or other tall vessel. Garnish with fresh mint sprigs.

The Healing Power of Huna (it's "Bar Noni!")

Yellow noni fruit comes from an evergreen primarily growing on the Pacific islands. Tahitians and Hawaiians used this fruit for food and various forms of medicine, both physical and spiritual. The kahunas of Hawaiian tribes knew the vast healing properties of noni as "huna" or "that which is hidden". In other words, they guarded noni's secret medicinal potency quite fiercely.

Today noni and its uncommonly odd flavor of juice survive on the islands from which it came. The straight fruit tastes tart, sour, and frankly a bit fetid. Therefore noni lives on mainly in superfruit blends. I use a Tahitian noni juice blended with blueberry and grapefruit. So you won't taste what tribesmen tasted, but you'll get some inflection of real Polynesian produce without triggering your gag reflex.

The maker boasts that it includes "powerful antioxidants, adaptogens, nutrients and phytonutrients to naturally boost energy levels, immune system function and overall health". Just leave it to me to dash that health store manifesto against the rocks with a good lashing of ethanol.

Tongan Holiday

1 oz Tahitian noni juice

1 oz mango nectar

1.5 oz Diplomatico or Brugal Anejo Rum

¾ oz white port

¾ oz vanilla simple syrup

2 dashes Bittermen's Krupnik Herbal Honey Bitters

Shake all ingredients with ice and strain over fresh ice (pebble, if possible) in a tulip glass. Garnish with skewered mango (fresh or dry).

Goosed Up

Gooseberries (a.k.a. golden berries) are closely related to currants. They start as green, veiny berries that are a bit too tart to eat. Once they ripen into an orange-yellow shade, they sweeten and become more agreeable. They actually look eerily like little plant-shaded eyeballs. Weird.

Your more interesting grocer's produce section will carry these for a long period while in season. But you can also find bottled gooseberry juice at Indian markets and other foreign food outlets. It enhances this effervescent botanical creation that citrus can't, while in essence fulfilling the same purpose—to balance the sweeter elements.

Golden Eye

1 oz freshly muddled gooseberry juice

1 oz Nolet's Silver Gin

½ oz mint simple syrup

¾ oz Caprano Bianco Vermouth

½ oz Don Ciccio & Figli Finochietto (Fennel) cordial

1-2 oz Prosecco or Cava

Muddle gooseberries in a shaker and then add all liquids but sparkling wine. Shake with ice and strain into a flute glass. Top with bubbly. Garnish with a rosemary sprig.

Golden Eye (left),
Tongan Holiday

New Jack(fruit) City

Jackfruit became the new hotness a year or two ago, it seems. In the current scene, it's become the vegan's refuge as a meat replacement in tacos and other interesting comestibles. And to my pleasant surprise, it works a treat that way. But I, of course, lean towards its liquid applications.

Being that it hails from southern India, Sri Lanka, Indonesia, and the Philippines, jackfruit pairs well with other silky sweet tropical fruits. It needs to be quite ripe to render sweetness and texture, so I like to use jarred jackfruit preserves. This also bypasses the sometimes difficult search for fresh fruit, as well as added labor.

Tropicalia

1 heaping bar spoon of Kamayan Langka jackfruit

1.5 oz Cazadores Blanco Tequila

½ oz Chairman's Reserve Spiced Rum

½ oz mango juice

½ oz lime juice

1-2 oz Ting (or other grapefruit soda)

Muddle jackfruit and juices in a shaker tin. Add spirits and ice. Shake and strain mixture over fresh ice in a tall Collins or zombie glass. Top with the soda. Garnish with skewered cubes of jackfruit.

Lassi Come Home

While lassi originated in India, you can find it fairly readily. Often enjoyed as a dessert, lassi combines dahl (yogurt), water, spices and often fruit. Mango lassi typically enjoys preferred status at many Indian restaurants. Though I do tend to avoid dairy cocktails, lassi helps me overcome this aversion. Hopefully you'll enjoy this modest tribute, too.

Gunpowder Milkshake

1.5 oz Mango Lassi

1.5 oz Pusser's Gunpowder Rum

½ oz Clement Mahina Coco

½ oz Cherry Heering

½ oz fresh lime juice

½ oz demerara simple syrup

Shake everything with ice and strain over fresh ice or pebble ice in a snifter or tulip glass. Sprinkle with nutmeg or cinnamon powder.

Optional: Drizzle blackstrap or Goslings rum float on surface before sprinkling spice.

Gunpowder Milkshake (left),
Tropicalia

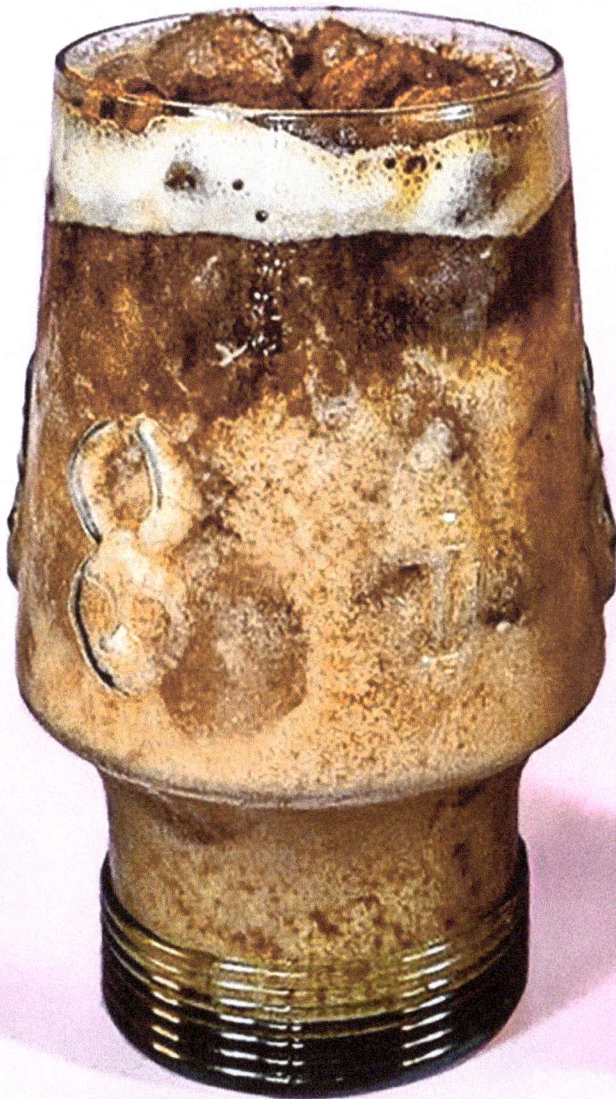

Breezeway Boogie

This drink comes as an awkward apology to Spike Marble, host of the Spike's Breezeway Cocktail Hour show and frontman extraordinaire for The Hula Girls. We both attended the 2022 Hukilau tiki festival. My bar's festival schedule kept me from attending his remote recording for the Breezeway show, which normally tapes at his home tiki bar. My wife attended the Hukilau taping as an emissary, and texted me for dazzling questions to ask during his Q&A session.

I responded "Ask him if he plans to do a cocktail called The Murderqueen" (the persona of his girlfriend and pinup model). Perhaps the Florida heat stroke overtook my wife, but she

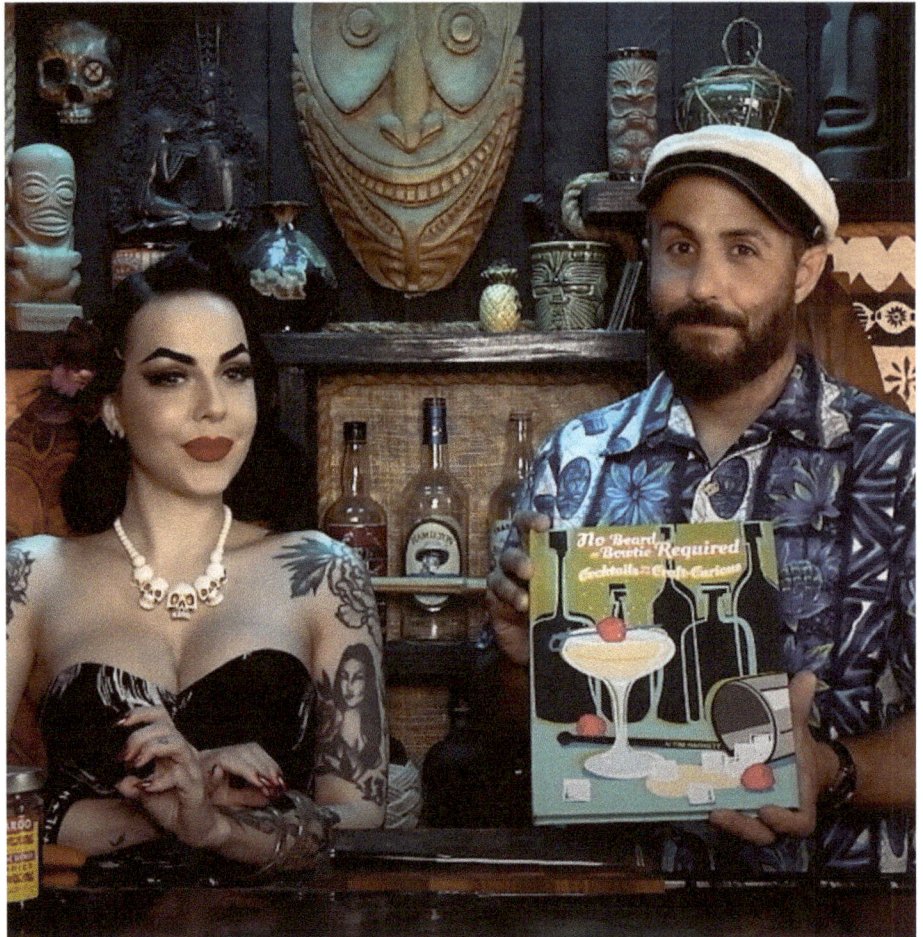

The Murderqueen and Spike Marble

came back with this story asserting that The Murderqueen was his dog. And I did know they owned a very cute dog from their Instagram posts. Still, it seemed a truly odd name for a lap dog with a very comfortable domestic background.

I argued that this was indeed a female human's name, but she wasn't having it. So later I ran into Spike at a festival afterparty and reluctantly inquired, "so my wife tells me the Murderqueen is your dog?". He assured me that the royal murderess was indeed his girlfriend. I looked a proper ass clown and quietly Irish-exited the conversation, and the building where it took place.

So these recipes hopefully apologizes sufficiently for the faux pas. We did briefly chat about Murderqueen cocktail ideas later. Spike said it has to be red. He dislikes Campari so that's off the table. Being that Spike devotes a great deal of research into heritage tiki recipes, I aimed at a blood-red tiki drink structured similarly to the 1944 Mai Tai, with a murderous helping of overproof rums. Blood orange juice also lends rather predictably to its dark red hue.

Murderqueen I
tart, funky and somewhat less than subtle

1 oz Hampden Estate Overproof dark rum

1 oz Wray & Nephew Overproof silver rum

½ oz Solerno blood orange cordial

½ oz Luxardo sour cherry syrup

½ oz pure pomegranate juice

½ oz pink grapefruit juice

¼ oz orgeat

2 dashes Peychaud's Bitters

Murderqueen II
sweeter sneak attack

1 oz Plantation OFTD Overproof Rum

1 oz Rum Bar Overproof silver rum

½ oz Malfy Aranciata (blood orange) Gin

½ oz raspberry syrup

½ oz pure pomegranate juice

½ oz pink grapefruit juice

¼ oz orgeat

2 dashes Peychaud's Barrel Aged Bitters

Murderqueen III
a happy medium between I and II

1 oz Plantation OFTD Overproof Rum

1 oz Rum Bar Overproof silver rum

½ oz Solerno blood orange cordial

½ oz Mathilde or Giffard Framboise (raspberry) cordial

1.5 oz pink grapefruit juice

¼ oz orgeat

¼ oz passion fruit syrup

4 heavy dashes Peychaud's Bitters

Shake all ingredients with ice and strain over pebble ice in a Mai Tai or oversize rocks glass. Garnish with a mint sprig and a gummy heart candy skewered on a cocktail sword.

Chase the Dragon

Dragonfruit deterred me for the longest time. Once I saw it on bottles of low cost flavored rums and vodkas, I assumed it was just stupid and gimmicky. Then I happened upon actual yellow and red dragronfruits at the West Side Market. I bought both varieties and started playing around, not realizing they both cost quite a bit.

I discovered that the red dragonfruit had very little flavor. Muddling this fruit produces a unique, almost creamy texture. However, it also produces a lot of seeds that must be strained out or endured clogging a straw. If you plan to experiment with real dragonfruit, the yellow variety of this fruit is immensely more sweet and flavorful.

Oddly enough, bottled natural dragonfruit exists at Whole Foods and other higher end grocery stores for a surprisingly affordable price.. So if you can deal with entitled champagne socialists blocking the aisles, you'll alternately save yourself the expense and hassle of juicing an uncooperative fruit.

The Horde of Balthromaw (a.k.a. Cha-Ching)

2 oz yellow dragonfruit juice (homemade or Sambazon brand)

¾ oz cinnamon syrup

¼ oz Cynar

½ oz fresh lime juice

1 oz Wray & Nephew Gold Rum

1 oz Japanese plum wine

2 Rainier cherries

Shake all ingredients with ice and strain over fresh ice in a tall Collins glass. Top with a splash of club soda. Garnish with two Rainier cherries on a bamboo skewer.

Sweet and Sour

Soursop fruit, also known as guanabana, thrives in the tropical regions of America and also the Caribbean. This prickly green fruit tastes more sweet and creamy than its appearance would suggest. Because of this, it is usually used as a coconut substitute in cocktails resembling Pina Coladas. I don't like these, nor getting caught in the rain.

Conversely, I think soursop remains far underutilized in more complex tropical cocktails. Good non-concentrate, unsweetened soursop juice can be found at more exotic markets or online. This concoction embraces the more obvious soursop flavor pairings. I encourage you to try using spare juice on some creations of your own.

The Ugly American

1 oz Nilo Soursop Juice

½ oz passion fruit cordial (Chinola, Giffard, Passoa)

1 oz dark rum

½ oz creme de banana (Giffard, Tempus Fugit)

½ oz vanilla syrup

¾ oz lime juice

Shake all ingredients with ice and strain over pebble ice in a highball glass. Garnish with pineapple leaves and lime.

Suck it, Sir Paul

Writing this segment of the book during summer, it seems inevitable for a true barfly's mind to drift towards a strawberry-accented creation. And bearing that in mind, many people would expect me to entitle either this segment or the drink "Strawberry Fields Forever". That clearly is not going to happen.

Jesus, the two Beatles that are still alive persist in torturing us with new recordings despite the staggering royalties they live on. And every damned generation can't seem to stop buying re-issues every year. You thought I had an issue with Phil Collins? I'd build a time machine to prevent the Beatles from being force-fed to the planet for six decades now.

So here's my reverse love song to a band that casts an endless shadow over all other musicians in history. Maybe a "Sinking Yellow Submarine" should come next . . .

Strawberry Fields on Fire

1.5 oz strawberry nectar

¾ oz jalapeno simple syrup

¾ oz Punt e Mes

¼ oz Hamilton Pimento Dram

1.5 oz Pimms #1 Cup

½ oz fresh lemon juice

Shake all liquids with ice. Heap a tall glass with pebble or crushed ice. Strain mixture over ice.

Hollow out the top of a full, fresh strawberry and nestle it in the ice. Add mint garnish. Drip lemon oil or inexpensive overproof spirit into strawberry and light it.

Strawberry Fields on Fire (left),
Ugly American

You Could Fall in Love with a Gorilla in that...

Some friends visited the bar on a slow evening while I stood behind the stick at the tiki bar. They tried some new fare on the menu, then suggested I try something with a bounty of concorde grapes they'd picked up on their route. Never one to stand down from a drink challenge, I accepted the offer.

You might think a tiki bar would limit the creative options, but in truth, all the rums and cordials surrounding me made this pretty easy. I arrived at the recipe below, with no knowledge how fresh grapes would interact with tropical spirits and syrups. Turns out it was pretty fucking magic.

Grape Ape

8-10 fresh concord grapes

2 oz aged white rum

¾ oz cinnamon simple syrup

`½ oz sweet orange cordial (Gran Gala, Cointreau)

½ oz dry vermouth

2 dashes ginger bitters

Muddle a small bunch of grapes in the bottom of a shaker, keeping them attached to stems. Add all liquid ingredients and shake with ice. Strain into a pilsner or Collins glass. Garnish orange peel and grape on a bamboo skewer or cocktail pick.

Gee your Hands Smell Terrific

Buddha's hand really does not lend itself well to a bar program due to its rarity and cost. So this drink might really fit the whole "cocktails for the couch" ethos more than any other in this book.

Buddha's hand looks like a small lemon with long, finger-like segments growing from it. It contains no fruit or pulp, but the peel and pulp are extremely fragrant and perfumey. This floral character sets it apart from other fruits in the citrus family. But you will likely need to seek it at Asian markets or posh organic grocers.

The fruit symbolizes good fortune and is commonly offered at the altars of Buddhist temples. If you find it, take it as a sign that you should use it for the equally noble religion of drinks. It makes an extremely floral simple syrup. Simply steep peels in warm simple in order to get the most from this rather expensive and rare fruit.

Red Right Hand

¾ oz Buddha's hand syrup

1.5 oz Pavan grape spirit

1.5 oz dry vermouth

¾ oz honey mix

4-5 raspberries

Muddle berries in a shaker with the honey mix. Add ice and the liquid ingredients and shake. Strain into a champagne flute. Cut an additional peel for garnish.

Grape Ape (left),
Red Right Hand

Chapter 8: The Flowers of Romance
Drinks from the Garden

Okay, all the macho guys . . . just leave the room. Skip this chapter. This is where you leave your silly preconceptions of masculinity at the door. If you're one of these assholes that makes me pour their Manhattan from a coupe into a rocks glass, then definitely skip this chapter. Any guy that feels immasculated when drinking their cocktails from stemware can fuck right off.

Sorry. This chapter got off to an ironically roid-ragey start, didn't it?

So yes, this delightful segment focuses on flowers and flowery herbs. And this is not to imply dressing up your drinks like a florist. I speak of flower and herb extracts in one form or another. A wide range of flowers go into bitters, syrups and even spirits. Flowers, for example, can share the stage with juniper and other botanicals in gin.

Flower "waters" also very effectively spark floral aromas and flavors in drinks, quite often without you even knowing. These "hydrosols" are the water-soluble aromatic compounds left over after oil-soluble aromas have been removed. These intensely flavorful liquids include the more common orange blossom and rose, and extend to the more exotic hibiscus and jasmine waters. Just a few drops of orange or rose give syrups like grenadine and orgeat their subtle floral pop.

Reading onward, you'll see that each cocktail in this chapter gets its distinctive zing from some form of flower or herb extraction—be it in the form of bitters, syrup, or spirit. As I'm writing this introduction, I'm still on the fence about using Elderflower. It's too overdone. Thank you, St. Germain and your overpriced fancy bottle that makes you feel bad about throwing it away . . .

Flowers for Algernon (left), The Improved Honeydripper

Garden Variety

There come times where you default to mixes that simply fit too naturally. It feels lazy and derivative and just . . . sort of dirty. This is how I feel when I use elderflower spirit. This cordial uses elder tree flowers to impart a very light grape-like floral note. It usually gets mixed with gin that damn well might have elderflower in it already.

As soon as St Germain hit the market, everyone fell in love with the stuff, even though all the cost was in the fancy bottle. Eventually elderflower liqueur inherited the name "bartender's ketchup". Even bars with the most blase' drink menus were doing gin and elderflower drinks. Elderflower plays well with other spirits, too.

I just feel like a copycat no matter how I use the stuff. I guess I should be glad a Victorian era cordial came close to eclipsing all the dumb vodka flooding the market.

I think elderflower could mix well with robust whiskies. This drink pairs it with a less aggressive base spirit—Basil Hayden Toast. This bourbon adds toasted rice into the mashbill, giving it good mixability for summer cocktails. I think it one-ups the original recipe that called for a cucumber-infused spirit.

The Improved Honeydripper

- 1.5 oz Basil Hayden Toast Bourbon
- ½ oz Amoretti Honeydew or 1883 Maison Routin Melon Syrup
- ¾ oz Bitter Truth Elderflower Spirit
- ¾ oz pink grapefruit juice
- 2 oz Italian sparkling lemon soda

Shake all ingredients except the soda with ice. Strain mixture in a flute glass. Garnish with grapefruit and cucumber.

Roses Rouges pour Moi

Sheesh, I'm using more French in this book than I should feel comfortable with. I don't even speak it. Google translate could be telling me to say trigger words for a brainwashed assassin and I'd have no goddamn idea. Moving on . . .

So again, France gives us a highly complex, floral spirit just begging for attention in cocktails. Fluer Charmante, literally translated as "charming flower", macerates blackcurrant, raspberry and cherry fruits, accented by natural violet, lavender, and jasmine. I mean, god damn, right?

Flowers for Algernon

- 1 oz Fluer Charmante
- 1 oz Reposado Tequila
- 1 oz pink grapefruit juice
- ½ oz bianco vermouth
- ½ oz agave syrup
- 2 dashes orange bitters
- Prosecco topper

Shake all but bitters with ice and strain the chilled mixture over fresh ice in a highball glass. Drip bitters on the drink surface. Garnish with a skewered grapefruit peel. Top with prosecco.

Pining for Good Drink

When gin naysayers complain about gin, they often moan about the "pine forest" assaulting their senses. This usually misinterprets the juniper that fronts the other botanicals in the gin.

As much as I enjoy pleasing guests who love good gin drinks, I might enjoy making the naysayer ilk suffer even more. So imagine my glee when I discovered that a respected Oregon microdistiller makes Douglas Fir Brandy—a spirit that makes an actual pine forest spirit. Take that, you moaning philistines . . .

This drink brings together a forestry of great pairings with the pine brandy—maple, sweet orange, fresh lemon, and the select botanicals that go into Hendrick's Lunar Gin.

Moon Over Willamette

¾ oz Clear Creek Douglas Fir Brandy

1 oz Hendrick's Lunar Gin

½ oz Cointreau

¾ oz maple syrup mix

½ oz fresh lemon juice

Shake all ingredients with ice and strain over a large format cube in a rocks glass. Lay a mint sprig and three pine nuts on the surface of the cube.

Running Spice across the Brooklyn Bridge

In the craft bartending racket, one tends to get bored pretty quickly unless someone makes a truly eyebrow-raising spirit. Thankfully producers like Jack From Brooklyn (JFB) Distillery smack the desk with a ruler to wake up fickle jerks like me from time to time.

JFB resurrected a 500 year old spirit recipe by bringing exotic ingredients from many corners of the globe to their doorstep. First and foremost is the Moroccan hibiscus, which is blended with Brazilian clove, Indonesian cassia, and Nigerian ginger. The spice balances out the floral sweetness of this crimson red spirit.

And yes, I know this drink has orgeat and it's not in the orgeat chapter.

Morocco Molli

1 oz Sorel

1 oz Rittenhouse Rye

½ oz Giffard Orgeat

1 oz pear nectar

¼ oz Meletti Amaro

2 dashes Aztec Chocolate/ Mole bitters (Bittermen's, Dashfire, etc.)

Shake ingredients with ice and strain over fresh ice in a Collins glass. Garnish with Candied ginger on a skewer.

Morocco Molli (left),
Moon over Willamette

Spanish Bombs (left),
Elder Kettle

Tunel of Love

Tunel de Mallorca might prove an elusive spirit in most states, but a five-minute internet search can solve this issue. And you won't regret this oddball's presence in your home bar, purely for mixing with gin, if nothing else.

Rosemary, chamomile, mint, fennel and marjoram give Tunel its unique herbal flavor. These all inspired the cocktail below. It's made with as many other spirits and juices that are also native to Spain.

Spanish Bombs

¾ oz Tunel de Mallorca

1.5 oz Mahon Gin

½ oz Mandarin or Clementine orange citrus juice

½ oz Pomelo or pink grapefruit juice

½ oz mint simple syrup

1-2 oz brut cava

Shake all ingredients except the cava with ice. Strain over fresh ice in a pilsner glass. Garnish with a fresh mint sprig. Top with cava.

Teabagging

I found jasmine flower water pure happenstance. I bought it without hesitation as jasmine would surely propel the love affair with flower waters that rose and orange blossom had sparked.

Afterwards I discovered that finding flavor pairings for jasmine is really tough. I could take the easy route and just drip it on top of an obvious gin drink. And while researching, I found every information source went straight to jasmine green tea and then basically hit a wall.

So this little number represents your humble author starting a drink with a compatible tea, then building its way up to jasmine flower water.

Elder Kettle

1 oz English blackcurrant tea

½ oz elderflower spirit

1 oz Pimms No 1 Cup

½ oz simple syrup

¾ oz tangerine juice

2 drops Fee Brothers Jasmine Flower Water

Shake all ingredients except flower water with ice and strain mixture into a chilled coupe. Drip flower water into the glass. Garnish with an edible flower.

Zuzu's Petals (left),
Moonracker

Petal to the Metal

Flower petal gins gained some attention in recent years, with new varieties of Japanese gins leading the charge. Gins like Hendrick's and Nolet's have used rose petals for years as well. But I don't recall previously seeing rose or other flower petals so much at the forefront of a gin's character that it gives the spirit a pink hue. These gins get good marks as long as they do their steeping or infusions naturally.

Personally I like Dillon's Rose Gin from Canada or Dorothy Parker from Brooklyn Distilling. Other producers make equally good examples. These give you the floral element you might otherwise seek from rose water, which can quite easily overpower a drink. Give this one a spin using a good spirit. If you must resort to vodka, use Ketel One Botanicals Grapefruit and Rose. Just don't tell me about it.

Zuzu's Petals

1 oz Dillon's or Dorothy Parker Rose Gin

½ oz Luxardo

¾ oz Mathilde Framboise

½ oz tangerine juice

½ oz simple syrup

1-2 oz Jam Jar sweet white or other moscato

Shake all but the wine with ice. Strain into a flute glass. Top with moscato, to taste. Garnish with dried rose or other flower petals.

Moonrise Kingdom

Korea considers Seollal or the lunar new year one of its most important holidays. Hell, the party lasts three days. So isn't it curious that I discovered Maesil-cha (Korean plum tea) about the same time that Hendrick's Lunar Gin was released? Nuff said.

Moonraker

1.5 oz Maesil-cha Korean plum tea

1.5 oz Hendrick's Lunar Gin

1 oz Copper & Kings Immature (or other unaged) Brandy

¾ oz Monin Lemongrass Syrup

¾ oz fresh lemon juice

Shake all with ice and strain over fresh ice in a tall glass. Garnish with sprigs of lemongrass.

Chapter 9: Your Cordial Invitation
Cocktails inspired by Cordials

As much as base spirits provide a foundation for most cocktails, I often get more excited about the cordials that usually round out and often tame those spirits. Creative mixologists can also build great lower proof drink recipes using cordials, vermouths, and other low-strength ingredients.

Think about it. Your average spirits store has entire aisles of your classic base spirits. Unfortunately, the largest aisle space usually goes to the flavorless blight on cocktailing—vodka. Then you have your gin, rum and whiskies taking up the lion's share of the leftover space.

And while each of those spirits carries its distinct flavor, you can usually interchange, for example, one dry gin for another. Don't get me wrong, people creating recipes choose specific spirits for a reason. But if I'm snowed in at home and only have one dry gin, chances are good it's going to work in a drink calling for a different dry gin.

Now, just for laughs, look at the "Cordials" section of your liquor store. Odds are pretty damned good that it's going to be a partial aisle. And a good portion of that section will be filled with unspeakable bottom-shelf bile that shall remain unnamed. This saddens me, as the world produces some truly stellar cordials that mostly remain local to their points of origin.

Be that as it may, we can rejoice in the good cordials that do make it to most stores that are worth visiting. Most of these don't share shelf space with the high proof spirits. Make it a point to locate the low proof section of your local shop and I guarantee you'll find other naturally-infused, quality spirits like Giffard and Ferrand. These often come from French producers that use good base spirits and ingredients.

I hope I don't need to say this out loud, but leave the obviously gimmicky, chemically-tinted nonsense for the bars that make flavored shots. Reading onward, you'll see I specify certain brands of cordials for each recipe. This usually represents what I can find in my local stores or online. Just be smart about any substitutions.

For example, if a recipe says to use Giffard Creme de Cacao, don't presume to swap it out for any gross chocolate liqueur. Frankly, if you're doing that, you should probably donate this copy of your book to your local library.

Viva Michigan

A Michigan blueberry spirit inspired this drink. The state gets more renown for its distinctively sharp cherries, which do accent several spirit creations from across the state. However, blueberry cordials are quite rare. Unique cocktail purveyors like Max's South Seas Hideaway in Grand Rapids knew this; they even figured out how to make it work in tiki drinks.

Iron Fish makes an exceptional blueberry spirit, among many other unique cordial expressions. You can find other blueberry cordials, however, from other microdistillers.

Blue Suede Lagoon

- ½ oz Iron Fish Blueberry cordial (or other respectable brand blueberry spirit)
- ½ oz Tempus Fugit Gran Classico
- 1.5 oz Sagamore Spirit Rye
- 2 dashes Bittercube Blackstrap Bitters

The High Hat (left),
Blue Suede Lagoon

Stir all ingredients with ice and strain into a chilled coupe. Garnish with blueberries on a cocktail skewer.

Mission to Maarten

Sint Maarten in the Caribbean crams a lot of history and cultures into a very small amount of island real estate. Originally colonized by both the French and the Dutch, this place now plays host to over 100 nationalities. Funnily enough, the French and Dutch fought over it for quite some time before it became the tourist paradise known today. They penned 12 treaties over the territory and violated them all.

Equally quizzical is the wild guavaberry that grows in the hot center of Sint Maarten. Hand-harvested bushels of these are macerated in a locally-made aged rum base. The main distiller here also makes other macerations with local tropical fruits. The wild guavaberry expression probably offers the truest flavor of the island. And on the shelves of more diversified stores, you can sometimes find it in the US.

The High Hat

- 1 oz Sint Maarten Wild Guavaberry cordial (sub sloe gin or Sorel if unavailable)
- 1 oz Chairman's Reserve Spiced Rum
- 1 oz blood orange juice
- ½ oz falernum
- ½ oz fresh lime juice

Shake ingredients with ice and strain over pebble ice in a tulip glass. Garnish with guava slice on a cocktail pick.

Big in Japan

Ever since determining that my perfect and preferred classic cocktail is the Mai Tai, I've launched a mission to conjure new and interesting riffs. As stated in my previous book, this superbly versatile cocktail works well with most base spirits: rum, tequila, gin or rye to name a few.

This version embraces the gin version with whispers of flavors from the far east. It works well with Roku Japanese gin, but will also work with other expressions such as Nikka Coffey Gin or 135 East Gin. The drier botanical half is balanced out using sweeter Japanese plum gin, along with lychee and orange cordials. It makes a lazy day in the summer shade quite a zen moment.

Ironically, I named it after a giant glowing monster that destroys entire cities and terraforms the earth for larger, incoming alien conquerors.

Maitaiju

- 1 oz Roku Japanese gin
- ½ oz Haketsuru or Choya plum wine
- ½ oz Giffard Lichi-Li
- ½ oz Pierre Ferrand dry orange curaçao
- ¾ oz lime
- ½ oz orgeat

Shake all ingredients with ice and strain over fresh ice in a Mai Tai or large rocks glass. Garnish with a skewered Lychee fruit and a fresh mint sprig.

From the House of Tabu

Some of those drinks that bring you the most pride come from challenges. Specifically those challenges from guests to invent a great new cocktail while they wait. Or perhaps when visiting a friend's home bar, where you must make something using only those ingredients they have on-hand.

One such moment was born from an invitation to the House of Tabu, an amazing home tiki bar that our friend Ken Howlewczynski built. This bar inspires his tiki sculpting business of the same name, and also serves as a muse for his tiki magazine Exotica Moderne.

This cocktail owes its origin to our invitation to his little tropical hideaway in South Bend, Indiana. We engaged in a "chopped" style challenge to create a drink for the magazine's upcoming issue.

After about six warmup drinks, this cocktail emerged from my rum-addled brain. In keeping with the theme of this chapter, its inspiration bloomed from a drunken desire to marry apricot cordial with an aperitif and funky Jamaican rum.

The Den of Iniquity

- 1 oz Hamilton Pot Still Jamaican Rum
- ½ oz Rothman & Winter or other apricot liqueur
- ½ oz Aperol
- 1 oz cinnamon syrup
- ½ oz fresh lime juice
- 1 oz mango juice

Shake all ingredients with ice and strain over fresh ice in a Mai Tai or large rocks glass. Garnish with a blood orange wheel or orange peel.

Brizard of Odd

When it comes to spirits, you have to love France. Set aside your (or the rest of the planet's) distaste for their bloody mindedness. France makes unparalleled brandy, armagnac, renowned cognacs, and in my mind, probably the world's best cordial spirits. Oh yeah, and I hear the wine is good. They also protest traffic legislation with outlaw gusto.

One such cordial producer, Marie Brizard, makes my job easier. They produce a centuries-old recipe for anisette liqueur, and a pretty vast portfolio of curiously unfamiliar flavors. Some of these include bergamot, mandarin, and the yuzu spirit included below.

Yuzu ponies up an intense tartness that essentially takes it off the table for anything other than a zesting or souring agent. While it has its own unique aroma and flavor, it bears some resemblance to oro blanco grapefruit and Eureka lemon. The spirit version saves you the hassle of hunting down east Asian citrus juice, while still capturing the flavor essence. Yuzu fruits cannot be imported into the US, so take it as you can.

Pinyin Graffiti

- 1 oz Marie Brizard Yuzu spirit
- 1 oz Ransom Old Tom Gin
- ½ oz mango nectar
- ½ oz cinnamon syrup
- 1 oz Oribe Mamaki Tea
- ¾ oz Bianco vermouth
- 2 dashes Fee Brothers Rhubarb Bitters

Shake all ingredients with ice and strain over fresh ice in a tall Collins or zombie glass. Garnish with a fresh mint sprig.

Pinyin Graffiti (left), The Den of Iniquity

With your Kind Persimmon

Good cocktails often owe their origin to great distilling cities and states. This drink helps me fondly recall a trip to Chicago, which included a brief side quest to Milwaukee. Both cities and states have great distillers like Death's Door, Few Spirits, Leatherbee . . . the list unravels for a while. The list also includes the fine producers below.

This drink tips my hat to some outstanding Chicago distillers, while acknowledging Wisconsin's penchant for brandy. I confess this one does not offer much wiggle room, as some of the spirits don't have close equivalents of which I'm aware.

Apfelouge

¾ oz Apologue Persimmon Cordial

¾ oz Koval Oat Whiskey

¾ oz Dark Matter Cold Brew

¾ oz apple brandy

2 dashes Bittercube Trinity Bitters

Stir all ingredients with ice and strain into a chilled coupe glass. Garnish with a dried or fresh persimmon cube or brandied cherry on a bamboo skewer.

Dead Seeds & the Dirty Ground

Once I discovered a celery spirit exists, I had to make something with it. Even if it meant an extensive internet search to get it to the doorstep. My mind went straight to a savory, vegetal drink. Honestly it could lend a vegetal slant to a traditional gin martini. Maybe in a later chapter . . .

I'll just leave that next to a huge, steaming bowl of foreshadowing . . .

Anyhow, this one just made me think of dirt, in a good way. It's full of root plants, seeds, and earthy spices. I think an upwardly mobile hippie would enjoy it. Until I slap him and yell "lose the patchouly you sellout prick!"

Shallow Grave

1 oz Apologue Celery Root spirit

1 oz Real McCoy 3 Year Rum

¼ oz Falernum spirit (Velvet or other)

½ oz fresh lemon juice

½ oz carrot juice

½ oz ginger syrup

6 drops saffron water

2 dashes ginger bitters

Shake everything with ice and strain over a large format cube in a large rocks glass. Lay a celery leaf on the cube surface.

Shallow Grave (left),
Apfelouge

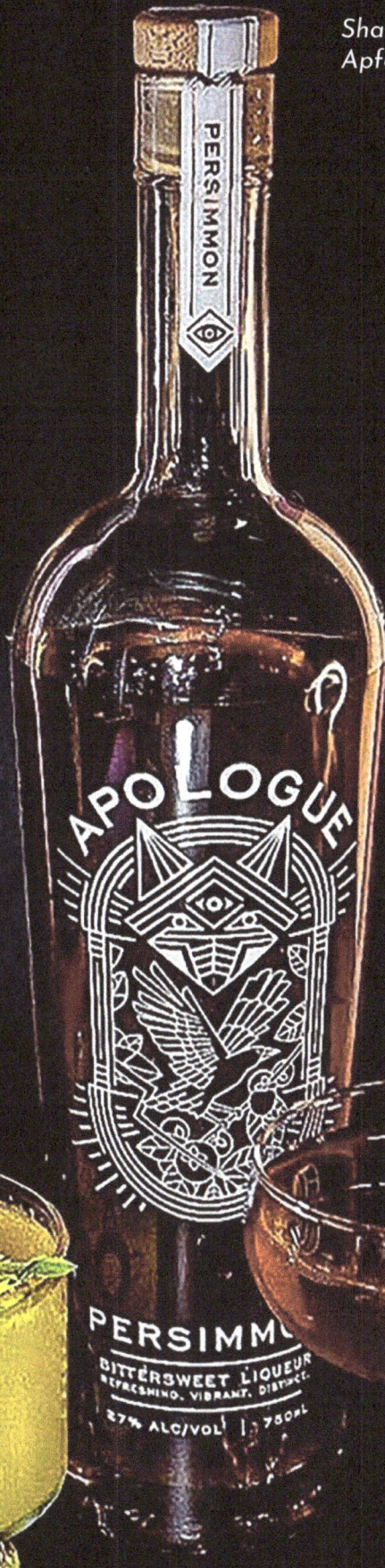

Gag Me with a Berry

My fondness for Apologue clearly defies measure. A distillery that devotes itself to such unique cordial spirits certainly stands out in a market saturated with traditional base spirit portfolios. Hell, their Aronia spirit just might be the most singularly odd and delightful in their lineup.

Aronia berries also go by the name "chokeberry", perhaps due to the reaction one has upon tasting them. They are tart and earthy, unlike the more accessible and popular berries we enjoy like blueberries. And though they look a bit like blueberries, you won't find them growing in the backyards of the midwest. They mainly grow on shrubs in wet swamp climates. They really only make it to the frozen sections of posh grocers where champagne socialists get their antioxidant fixes.

So why make a spirit with this berry? And further to that, actually make it good? I don't know, but Apologue did it. So in my book, it deserves attention in a cocktail. This creation takes its name from the central character in Chuck Palahniuk's *Choke*.

Victor Mancini

1 oz Apologue Aronia spirit

1 oz Sipsmith Strawberry Gin

½ oz Luxardo

¾ oz fresh lime juice

¾ oz honey mix

Shake all ingredients with ice and strain the chilled mix into a chilled coupe. Garnish with blueberries on a bamboo skewer.

Rescued from Obscurity

If you read the earliest bartender guides, you sometimes see drinks calling for extinct spirits. Take Pimm's for example. Did you know there were several numbered variations on this spirit, each called "cups"? Today only the basic Pimm's "No. 1 Cup" survives. Sure it delights the senses, but just imagine how swell all those other spirits might have tasted.

Another bygone spirit has evaded American shelves for many decades—Amer Picon. The bittersweet Picon apéritif still lives on in its native France but disappeared long ago outside Europe. The distinct orange flavor set Amer Picon apart from its contemporaries, which were primarily Italian herbal spirits. The pervasive orange peel was accented with gentian and cinchona, hence the French descriptor "amer", meaning "bitter".

A very select few ambitious distillers have thankfully resurrected the Amer Picon style. Golden Moon Distillery in Colorado reproduced a recipe from the 1830s. New Liberty Distilling in Pennsylvania also created a throwback spirit called American Picon, using Napa Valley Cabernet, neutral spirit, cinchona and bitter orange peel to replicate the Picon flavor profile.

Until now, Italy's Amaro Nonino and Amaro CioCiaro came closest to the Amer Picon flavor. If the above-mentioned tributes to Picon remain out of reach, these substitutions will work in this mixture.

Since we're getting all fancy and weird and French again, I'm throwing Armagnac into the mix too. Don't hate me when you have to look for this and pay for it. A Solid Cognac will work as well.

Picon Sidecar

¾ oz Picon or substitute spirit

1 oz Armagnac Casterade (or a reputable Coganc)

½ oz Luxardo Sour Cherry Syrup

¾ oz fresh lemon juice

Shake all but the bitters with ice and strain over fresh ice in a rocks glass. Express a lemon peel over the drink surface and add the peel to the glass. Drip Peychaud's Bitters over the ice.

Straight Outta Guangdong

Discovering weird cordials in the low proof section of the shop can sometimes be inspiring. You come across spirits you never thought existed, or never really conceived as being something that would even work. Case in point—lychee spirits.

Lychee is a quite sweet, mushy white fruit. It's quite an unmistakable flavor, so it rather becomes the "name above the title" kind of drink ingredient. Soho lychee tends to be most common, with Marie Brizard perhaps a close second. I'd recommend seeking out Giffard Lichi-Li, cited in this recipe. Other brands are out there, but I've no idea if they're good.

This mixture pals up lychee with some very good bedfellows—blackberry, lemongrass, and lemon. It defaults to what I consider a lazy choice of base spirit—white rum—but frankly it plays really well with everything. Blackberry syrup alone mingles well with everything else here, but if you can find or make an herbal blackberry syrup with basil, lemongrass, or tarragon, this added plant component will help further balance the sweetness.

Stagger Li (left), Picon Sidecar

Stagger Li

1 oz Kiyomi Japanese Rum (any reputable Caribbean silver also works)

½ oz blackberry syrup (preferably Western Fruit Exchange Blackberry Tarragon)

½ oz Giffard Lichi-Li

1 oz Giffard coconut syrup

¾ oz fresh lime juice

Shake all ingredients with ice and strain over fresh ice in a tall Collins or zombie glass. Garnish with a skewered Lychee fruit (if available) and brandied cherry.

Ostergrog (left),
The Prime Minister of Funk

Strange Fruit

In the previous chapter, I complained at great length over the commonality of elderflower spirit. Quite to the contrary, the berries that also come from elder trees have a much more exciting afterlife in the spirit world. Thank goodness for the cordial distillers that make spirits with strange fruit.

Rothman & Winter amped that magic up to the stratosphere with their elderberry cordial. It gets this amazing marzipan aroma from the addition of rowanberry, red currant and aronia berries. It's unlike any cordial you'll likely experience in your lifetime, and blends very well with virtually any base spirit.

Almost to prove its magical versatility, I felt compelled to put these alpine berry flavors in a tropical concoction. This grog also offers a hint of walnut spirit from the same Austrian family that makes the R&W cordials.

Ostergrog

1 oz Rothman & Winter Elderberry cordial

1 oz El Dorado 3 Rum

1 oz Pusser's Rum

1 oz Santa Cruz Apricot Mango organic juice

¼ oz Nux Alpina

½ oz honey mix

Shake all ingredients with ice and serve over ice in a large rocks glass or short highball glass. Garnish with a skewered mango slice or lime wheel.

Hogo Rising

Though rum provides the base for this spirited drink, the cordials steal the spotlight. It calls for orange curacao and ginger spirits with above-average intensity. It works with equivalent spirits of average fervor, but do try to use their more athletic counterparts. They're good to keep around for other drinks too.

Oddly enough it didn't hit me until writing this section, but the mixture below comes frightfully close to an El Presidente. Happy accident, I promise. This drink, however, kicks out more "hogo" or Jamaican funky flavors and aromas.

The Prime Minister of Funk

1.5 oz Hampden Estate 8 Year Rum

½ oz white wine reduction

½ oz Copper & Kings Destillaire Intense Orange Curacao

½ oz Barrow's Intense Ginger spirit

1 bar spoon craft grenadine

Stir all ingredients with ice and strain into a chilled coupe. Garnish with a Luxardo cherry and lime peel on a bamboo skewer.

A Bastard with an Identity Crisis

The classic Suffering Bastard cocktail arrived on the tiki scene in a sideways path. The original came from the 1940s, when trained chemist Joe Scialom turned to bartending. He slung drinks at the Long Bar in Cairo, entertaining British WWII soldiers often suffering from hangovers.

Joe's original version of the Suffering Bastard combined gin, brandy, lime, ginger beer and aromatic bitters. He formulated this simple and gentle mix to help relieve soldiers from the prior night's frivolities. Not too long after, Trader Vic introduced a Suffering Bastard on his menu. He even commissioned a special tiki mug for it, depicting what appeared to be a moai holding his forehead in agony.

Trader Vic engaged in various and mild forms of creative thievery just like anyone who came along after Don the Beachcomber. Usually he made riffs on previously invented tiki drinks. But in this odd case, he slapped the name "Suffering Bastard" on a completely different drink. The Vic version was basically his house Mai Tai with an extra ounce of rum. Vic's rendition did more to inflict suffering than its namesake, boasting 3.5 oz of spirits vs the original's 2 oz potion.

I can't say what convinced me to do this, but this drink marries the strength of Trader Vic's version with some of the main flavors of Scialom's original. It also enabled me to use the Trader Vic brand macadamia nut liqueur, which lives in that sweet and inexpensive realm I tend to avoid. But seriously, who else makes a macadamia spirit?

Kurious Oranj

½ oz 1883 Maison Routin Blood Orange Syrup

1 oz Bacardi Cuatro 4 Year Rum

1 oz Tiki Lovers White Rum

½ oz Trader Vic's Macadamia Nut Liqueur

½ oz Laird's Applejack or craft apple brandy

¾ oz lime juice

2 dashes Bittermens Elemakule Tiki Bitters

2 oz ginger beer

Shake all ingredients except ginger beer with ice and strain over fresh ice (pebble, if possible) in a large goblet. Top with ginger beer. Add a nugget of dry ice, mint sprig and a spent lime shell.

Whoopsie Daisy

Daisy cocktails taste wonderful, though many don't know what they are. Very few even put the term "daisy" in the name. Basically daisies blend 2 ounces of high proof spirit with citrus juice and sweetener, then get a small dose of bubbles from club soda. Orange cordial originally sweetened these cocktails, but grenadine gradually took its place early in the 20th century.

When I discovered the herbal cherry spirit Mount Rigi, my mind went straight to a daisy for some reason. This drink builds upon bonded brandy, while mingling clear creme de cacao with the herbal cherry flavors of Mount Rigi. Traditionally you serve a daisy in a metal julep cup, though a highball glass will work just as well.

Daisy Chainsaw

½ oz Mount Rigi herbal cherry spirit

½ oz Giffard or Tempus Fugit Creme de Cacao

1 oz Sacred Bond Brandy

¾ oz fresh lemon juice

½ oz Luxardo sour cherry syrup

1-2 oz club soda

Shake all liquids except club soda with ice. Strain over ice in a julep cup filled with pebble ice. Garnish with skewered lemon peel and dark cherry. Top with club soda.

Daisy Chainsaw (left), Banned in DC

Aperitvo for Destruction

Washington DC houses a wonderful distillery called Don Ciccio & Figli. This special producer focuses on long-forgotten aperitif and digestif spirits of Italian heritage. Quite often these lean a little sweeter and more approachable than their highly bitter counterparts like Campari and Fernet Branca. They also play very well indeed in cocktails.

One of my favorites among their impressive portfolio is Karkade, a medium-bitter aperitivo made with hibiscus since the turn of the 20th century. Hibiscus most often pops up in the tiki drink world, mainly as a floral sweetener or sometimes a cordial. Karkade let me embrace this heritage while giving an herbal accent to a new tropical cocktail. In essence, it blew down a wall that previously shorted out my creative synapses.

Banned in DC

¾ oz Don Ciccio & Figli Karkade Aperitivo

¾ oz Mathilde Peche cordial

1 oz Hamilton 86 Demerara Rum

¾ oz honey mix

¾ oz key lime juice

2 dashes Bittercube Blackstrap Bitters

Shake all ingredients with ice and serve over pebble ice in a tulip glass. Garnish with edible orchid or dried hibiscus flower and skewered peach cubes.

Wake up, Thyme to Die

The real inspiration for this cocktail lies with Bigallet, a producer I have lauded more than once in this very book for their outstanding and versatile spirits. I found out Bigallet makes a thyme cordial, which to my knowledge, no one else does. So of course it made a quick transition that went from web searching, to clandestine mail order services, and into the pages of this book.

Again, savory cocktails have always proven one of my shameful weaknesses. But the herbaceous nature of the Bigallet Thyme spirit led me to the artichoke-based Cynar, which pairs up as famously well with blackberry and honey. So the drink turned out to be pretty easy to conjure. I hope you'll agree if you manage to find Bigallet in your travels.

Chokehold

1 oz Bigallet Thyme cordial

½ oz Cynar 70

¾ oz Giffard Creme de Mure

¾ oz lime juice

½ oz honey mix

Shake all ingredients with ice and strain over ice in a tall Collins glass. Garnish with fresh thyme and mint sprigs.

Chocolate Thunder

If you've read this far, you'll surely see that I've got no qualms revealing the dark corners of my fractured mind. Hopefully my checkered past helped along the drink creator in me, alongside the overzealous drink consumer that kills those inventive brain cells.

The rubble of childhood travails that made me an angry adult included weekly visits to a shrink that, frankly, didn't accomplish anything. But being that my kind analyst plied me into talking by holding our sessions at an ice cream parlor, I guess the road behind me isn't completely littered with potholes. And this wasn't just a Baskin-Robbins chain. It was a decades old establishment in Medina Square that made chocolate phosphates.

A couple of recent discoveries let me revisit this nugget of joy: Calpico and Marie Brizard chocolate cordial. While Calpico has been immensely popular in its native Japan for a century, only around the time of penning this book has Calpico gained traction in the cocktail world. This fermented milk beverage has light sweetness with a tangy zing resembling phosphate.

Meanwhile, the Marie Brizard cordial allowed me to bring in a good chocolate flavor without a cloying chocolate cream spirit. It's one of the few drinks I've brained up that solely uses cordials. I gussied it up with some other fun autumn flavors too.

Parlor Trick

1 oz Calpico concentrate

1 oz Marie Brizard Chocolate cordial

1 oz Laird's Applejack

½ oz Cherry Heering

½ oz unfiltered apple juice

3 dashes Angostura Bitters

Shake all ingredients with ice and serve over ice in a tall Collins or zombie glass. Garnish with two dark cherries.

Chokehold (left),
Parlor Trick

A Nice Pair

Sometimes the best liquid creations arise when you're called upon to pair drinks with food. When the bar enlisted me to do so for a supper club event, this drink unfolded from flavors that pair well with pork. Honestly, I stole relentlessly from a flavor wheel diagram for pork. And I felt so strongly it would work, I didn't even road test it before the dinner event.

Thank fucking god it did work, rather amazingly actually. I hope you agree. This took inspiration from the raspberry and cacao cordials that so lovingly shared a bed with pork belly.

Pearls for Swine

2 oz Old Grand Dad Bonded Bourbon

0.5 oz cold brew concentrate

0.5 oz Giffard Creme de Cacao

0.25 oz orgeat

0.25 oz Giffard Framboise

0.5 oz fresh lemon juice

Shake and serve over ice in a Mai Tai glass. Garnish with coffee beans on an orange wheel.

Chapter 10: Spirited Away
Full-Spirited Concoctions

This is where shit gets real. Basically, this chapter is taking away all the other stuff you get to play with when creating cocktails.

No juice, no syrups. Just spirits, bitters and the ice with which you chill them.

Cocktail bars call these "spirit-forward" drinks. I've always found this nomenclature a bit unsettling. To me it sounds like there's something lurking behind the spirits. I mean, not to start an argument on semantics. But why not just call them "full-spirited"? Hell, that's probably how you'll feel after two or three of them.

Two or three, heh. Yeah. I'm sure it will stop there . . .

The thing I like about this chapter is that it gets to show the nuances of spirits that sometimes get buried or belittled by other ingredients. It lets you experience the subtle flavors of things like secondary barrel-rested spirits like "ported whiskies" or sherry-rested Irish whiskies. Furthermore it demonstrates how spirits and bitters play really well with each other when chosen carefully.

It also ups the challenge on you when your creative palette is basically cut in half. If you live in a state where your spirits options are minimal, it gets even tougher.

To quote Deadpool, are you ready to get your fuck on? . . .

Ransoms (left),
Pardon My French
Manhattan

Ça Plane Pour Moi

Black Manhattans have admittedly been a bit overdone in recent years. But they taste so wonderful, I hope they never run their course. In its most basic form, this riff replaces the Manhattan's traditional vermouth with a more dark and herbal amaro.

This little number takes its name from one of my regulars, whose penchant for curse words sometimes rivals my own. It's evolved a little since I originally created it on the fly. It got its initial zing from Averna amaro and dry orange curacao, with mole bitters giving a dark chocolatey backbone..

I think the name more correctly describes this updated version, while giving it a little more "je ne sais quoi". The Bigallet China-China proves that the French can make amari with the best of them. And the creole bitters provide a bit of cajun kick. If I've done my job properly, you'll say "fuck, that's good". Don't say "sacre bleu!", that's too predictable. Maybe "merde!".

Pardon my French Manhattan

2 oz Russell's Reserve Bourbon

½ oz Bigallet China-China

½ oz Pierre Ferrand Dry Orange Curacao

2 dashes Bittermen's Truth Creole Bitters

Stir all ingredients with ice and strain into a chilled coupe glass. Garnish with a skewered orange peel and brandied cherry.

Ransom Notes

Ransom Spirits ranks among my favorite American distillers. I treasure every precious drop that they perfect in their stills. They make one of the most distinctive Old Tom gins, unusual and well-rounded whiskies, and even two great vermouths.

Below are a couple of love letters to my friends/enablers at Ransom. I'd have written these with newspaper clippings, but I can't afford the extra design work for so many fonts. These also both call for some unusual cordials—one made with celery root and the other with saffron.

The King's Ransom

1.5 oz Ransom Old Tom Gin

½ oz Apologue Celery Root spirit

1 oz Ransom Dry Vermouth

2 dashes Bar Keep Apple Bitters

Optional absinthe rinse

The Queen's Ransom

1.5 oz Ransom Whipper Snapper Oregon Spirit Whiskey (or a young, pot-distilled, malted-barley heavy bourbon)

0.5 oz Apologue Saffron Spice spirit

1 oz Ransom Red Vermouth

2 dashes Bar Keep Apple Bitters

If desired, using atomizer, rinse the ice inside a chilled coupe with an absinthe mist. Stir all ingredients with ice and strain into the coupe. Garnish with a skewered cherry.

Remain in Dark

Basil Hayden makes some very interesting stuff outside their core bourbon and rye. For example, they made the sadly limited Caribbean, which added a touch of blackstrap rum to their rye. The result was sublime. Whiskey purists stayed away from it, which modestly extended its brief availability to cocktail nerds like me. Admittedly, this spirit inspired me to add blackstrap rum to every rye-tai I make to this day.

Thankfully the Basil Hayden Dark Rye only teased at being a limited availability spirit. This version artfully blends in a pinch of California port. As long as Basil Hayden keeps it around, I'll keep using it for as many liquid inventions as my booze-addled brain can conjur.

Prince of Darkness

1.5 oz Basil Hayden Dark Rye

½ oz Casa Mariol Black Vermut

½ oz Riga Black Balsam

½ oz Luxardo Sangue Morlacco (or Cherry Heering)

2 dashes Dead Rabbit Orinoco Bitters

Stir all ingredients with ice and strain over a large format cube in a rocks glass. Garnish with a Luxardo cherry.

The Trinity Knot (a.k.a The Auld Triangle)

Where I'm from, the popular consciousness of Irish whiskey tends towards shots of Jameson and Powers. And while both distillers make some exceptional whiskies, their lackluster flagship spirits sadly get the most attention. These distillers survived the decimated market Prohibition caused, while smaller ones did not.

Today smaller brands rise from these ashes in surprising numbers. Most of these are robust, pot-distilled spirits. And many of them get added character from secondary aging in other types of spirit barrels. These include ex-sherry and rum casks. I fawned over Sexton and Slane Irish whiskies in my first book, and figured this book should sing more praises to the twenty-six counties.

Here are three amped-up Irish whiskey versions of the Manhattan. Why didn't anyone give this expression of the Manhattan its own name? A Manhattan made with any kind of Scotch is considered a Rob Roy. Maybe I should coin this style the James Joyce . . . or maybe Graham Norton.

These three expressions take inspiration from the trinity knot, a traditional ring design composed of three different colors of gold bands. The white gold band symbolizes friendship, the yellow gold loyalty, and the rose band love. Each utilizes a smaller Irish distillery whiskey that gains character from unique barrel aging.

Not bad for a yank.

Friendly Fire

- 2 oz Writer's Tears Irish Whiskey
- ½ oz Falernum spirit
- ½ oz Luxardo Bitter Bianco (or conventional Bianco vermouth, if needed)
- 2 dashes orange blossom water

Loyal to the Craic

- 2 oz Drumshanbo Single Pot Still Irish Whiskey
- ½ oz Madeira
- ½ oz Averna
- 2 dashes Dale DeGroff's Pimento Bitters

Love on the Rocks

- 2 oz Teeling Irish Whiskey
- ½ oz Lustau Rose Vermouth
- ½ oz Cointreau
- 2 dashes Dr. Emigrab's Dandelion & Burdock Bitters

For each, stir all ingredients with ice and strain into a chilled coupe glass. Garnish with an orange peel and cherry on a skewer.

Trinity Knot Cocktails

A Better 'Highlander' Sequel

Meritable Scotch is a tough sell in the cocktail world. The spirit usually costs a higher price than other base spirits, and mainly survives dwindling popularity as a neat spirit. Then you have your bracingly salty and peaty varieties that I think most Scotch lovers drink on a dare, as much as they would when taunted to eat haggis.

Some producers make solid single malts that cost less and are marketed as more mixable. But being a devoted fan of Highland single malts, I think a great opportunity for cocktails gets overlooked. Some really great, high age Highland malts often run the same price as the lauded bourbons that go into higher tier Manhattans and old fashioneds. And many of these enjoy secondary barrel aging in coveted casks used for spirits like Sauternes and Pedro Ximenez sherry.

God damn, I'm ready to lean into some fancy party liquor just writing this.

Dyed in the Wool

- 1.5 oz Glenmorangie Lasanta
- 0.5 oz heather honey
- 0.5 oz Rothman & Winter Pear cordial
- 0.5 oz Luxardo maraschino cordial
- 2 dashes Dr Adam Elmegirab Dandelion & Burdock Bitters

Stir all ingredients with ice and strain over a large ice cube in a rocks glass. Garnish with a dandelion flower or an edible flower variety.

The Martini Affair

In my first book, I carried on pretty mercilessly about what defines a martini. Strictly speaking, any interpretation should include gin as the base spirit, complimented by some form of aromatized wine (traditionally dry vermouth). A couple dashes of floral bitters never hurts either.

But just like Manhattans, this three-ingredient stroke of genius leaves loads of room for "improved" versions with different spirit modifiers. This is, after all, how we arrived at the splendiferous Martinez.

Below are some favorite inventions I whipped together for a seasonal martini menu a few years ago. Don't make these with vodka, god dammit.

Imperial Bedroom Martini

- ½ oz Bianco Vermouth
- ½ oz Luxardo Maraschino cordial
- 2 oz Plymouth Gin
- 2 dashes Rhubarb Bitters

Stir with ice and strain into chilled cocktail glass. Garnish with lemon twist on skewer.

Rose Tattoo

- 1.5 oz Plymouth Gin
- ½ oz Maurin Le Puy Quina
- ½ oz Lustau Rose Vermouth·
- 2 dashes Bittermen's Krupnik Honey Bitters

Stir with ice and strain into chilled cocktail glass. Garnish with cherry on a skewer.

Rising Sun Martini

2.5 oz Plymouth Gin

½ oz Ikkomon Mugi Shochu

2 dashes Plum Bitters

Stir with ice and strain into chilled cocktail glass. Garnish with persimmon cube on skewer.

Tom2 Martini (a.k.a. The Martommy)

¾ oz Uncle Val's Botanical Gin

¾ oz Hayman's Old Tom Gin

1 oz Red Vermouth

½ oz Pierre Ferrand Dry Orange Curacao

1 dash Jerry Thomas bitters

Stir with ice and strain into a chilled cocktail glass. Garnish with orange peel and cherry on a skewer.

Four Martini riffs

As Close as I'll Get to a Vineyard

Wines never appealed to me. The tannins made my mouth feel all pasty and the headaches the next day just steered me away. I barely saved enough brain cells to contain spirit knowledge, much less the enormity of wine styles, regions, and producers. To this day I'm glad I still work at a cocktail bar where I can say "we have a red and a white" and the wine conversation ends right there.

Then I discovered aromatized and fortified wines. Oh what a "dear diary" time in my life . . .

As long as it comes from a good producer, I can enjoy good vermouth, sherry, madeira, and sauternes all by themselves. Put these in bed with the right high proof spirits and we're talking alchemy, not just mixology. Without aromatized wine, I probably couldn't identify France or Spain on a globe.

This recipe favors the northern of these two wonderful nations. It gets a little zing of ginseng flavor from Americano to balance out the sweeter high proof spirits and cordials.

The French Connection

2 oz Oat or Wheat Whiskey (Koval Oat, Old Elk Wheat)

½ oz Sauternes

¼ oz Cointreau

¼ oz St George Americano

Stir all ingredients with ice and strain into a chilled coupe.

Chapter 11: National Anthem
Cocktails Inspired by International Flavor

on't worry. This chapter is not a fascist rallying cry. Though I do bear accusations of being borderline brown-shirt when it comes to my merciless campaign against vodka. I'd actually consider burning down a building to rid the world of this blight on the spirit world. With people inside it. What might scare you more is the number of bartenders that would willfully commit that arson alongside me.

On the less mass-murdery side, I hope you'll enjoy the multicultural celebration that this chapter really is. Its muse is spirits that either strongly represent their country of origin, or conversely, are completely opposite of what you'd expect from said country.

For example, Sweden and Norway brought aquavit to us. Imagine that these nations wanted to create their own gin, but the forward botanicals were either caraway or dill. Most of it stays in Scandinavia, and few brands make it outside those borders. The American distillers that bring these spirits to our domestic audience, to no surprise, mostly reside in Minnesota.

On the flipside, a spirit will come from the most unexpected corner of the globe. Stroh rum, for instance, hails from Austria. You'd imagine that a spirit so mired in Caribbean culture and climate should never emerge from so opposite a country. And in this case you'd be right. The stuff is merciless overproof muck. I guess I could have chosen a more positive example for context, but I just like to make fun of Stroh.

But oddly, you sometimes get great spirits from countries you'd imagine have no business making them. Take Paranubes Rum—it comes from Mexico but has all the funk and fury of a Jamaican overproof. Didn't see that one coming. Maybe if you read onward just a little bit, you'll find a cocktail where this spirit gets real cozy.

Seriously, go make some drinks. Something's gotta make this book interesting . . .

Left my Wallet in Karlovy Vary

The Czechs gave us the true original Pilsner beer, but few realize they also gave us the complex herbal spirit Becherovka. Loaded with flavors of cinnamon, clove, ginger and anise, it's sure to gain fandom among followers of amari and other herbal, bitter spirits. It might even become a favored shot among your local bar staff. Unless, of course, you live in a liquor control state like Ohio. Then it will quickly get delisted and just piss you off.

A Scandal in Bohemia

¾ oz Becherovka

½ oz blueberry cordial spirit or simple syrup

1 oz Hayman's or Plymouth Sloe Gin

¼ oz ginger syrup

¾ oz fresh lemon juice

Approximately 1-2 oz sparkling craft cider

Shake all but cider with ice and strain over fresh ice in a tall Collins glass. Top mixture with cider, to taste. Garnish with a flamed cinnamon stick.

Attack Ships on Fire off the Coast of Amalfi

Italy catches my attention in the most unexpected ways. Of course they rule the realm of Amari and deservedly so. But they also excel in some spirit categories that make you tilt your head a bit, like a confused Italian greyhound. Take their craft beer scene. Blips of wildly exotic and frankly amazing craft beers sneak out of Italy all the time.

Italian gin gets high marks too. Malfy, from the coastal region of Amalfi, makes great traditional gin. They also make some fun and literally colorful infusions. This drink uses their surprisingly sweet blood orange gin.

Blood in the Water

1 oz Malfy Con Arancia Gin

1 oz pomegranate juice

¼ oz Giffard Creme de Cacao

¾ oz Carpano Antica

2 dashes black walnut bitters

Stir all ingredients with ice and strain mixture over large ice cubes in a rocks glass. Tuck a blood orange wheel alongside the ice cube.

Blood in the Water (left),
Scandal in Bohemia

Lillehammer Calling

If this book didn't have at least one aquavit cocktail in it, I should be haunted by the spirits of Vikings dragging their entrails behind them. It's so fucking good. If I could relocate there and start a new career as the "aquavit trail" tour guide, I'd be on a plane ten minutes ago. Maybe I could even enlist as a zombie extra in the next Dead Snow film. I sure as hell wouldn't go for the anchovies.

Anyhow, this drink rounds up all the flavors that would make Ingmar Bergman rise from the grave. It also panders to the flavor playbook that such a caraway-forward spirit requires: Norwegian aquavit, coriander-heavy gin, Danish dark cherry spirit, and applejack from . . . um, New Jersey. Hey, you work with what you can get.

Ni har varit en fantastisk publik, prova lutfisken.

No Sleep til Oslo

¾ oz Hovding Norwegian Small Batch Aquavit

¾ oz Death's Door Gin

¾ oz Laird's Applejack

¾ oz Cherry Heering

2 dashes orange bitters

Stir all ingredients with ice and strain into a chilled cocktail glass. Garnish with a brandied cherry on a bamboo skewer.

The Italian Cousin of Galactus?

Recently a unique Italian spirit called Italicus reappeared to the rest of the world. In full name, "Italicus Rosolio de Bergamotto" exemplifies a little known (and frankly, forgotten) spirit called Rosolio from southern Italy. It falls into the aperitivo/aperitif category due to its secret blend of bergamot and other botanicals. But it is surprisingly sweet for a spirit that mingles with much more bitter relatives.

My mind goes straight to a white negroni style with Italicus. It's going to lean sweet, almost as though using a Genever gin. So the opposing spirits have to be drier in comparison. I've chosen another Italian gin (see Malfy in the previous recipes) called Moletto, which uniquely includes savory botanicals like tomato, rosemary and basil.

A Moment of Clarity

1 oz Italicus

1 oz Moletto Gin

1 oz La Quintinye Royal Extra Dry Vermouth

2 dashes Angostura Orange Bitters

1 dash Bar Keep Lavender Bitters

Stir all ingredients with ice and strain over a large format ice cube in a rocks glass. Garnish with a thin orange wheel or blood orange wheel.

Moment of Clarity (left),
No Sleep til Oslo

Chile vs. Peru (No, it's not Soccer)

Today Pisco comes from both Chile and Peru, though the founding country still hangs in debate. Peru argues that it originated there, as the country has a river, port, and valley named "Pisco". Regardless, both countries produce basically a grape brandy that share similar tastes. Peru ages it in neutral casks that render it colorless, while Chile matures it in barrels that give it a light amber color.

Taking no sides, Pisco deservedly earns its place in the Pantheon of classic cocktail spirits. I hope this creation deserves a fraction of the attention of its wonderful base spirit.

Pisco Volante

1.5 oz Macchu Pisco (for a Peruvian version) or Capel Pisco (for Chilean)

½ oz Chareau Aloe spirit

½ oz Marsala wine

¼ oz mint simple syrup

½ oz raspberry brandy

2 dashes lemon bitters

Stir all ingredients with ice and strain into a chilled coupe glass. Garnish with a single mint leaf.

It's not just for Punch anymore

Batavia Arrack van Oosten only appears on the back bars of pretty geeked out cocktail bars. Its parent, the Dutch East Indies Trading Company, played a great part in the sugar and spice trade centuries ago. It also helped Arrack's cousin rum to spread across the globe from the Caribbean. Like rum, it became a staple in the earliest forms of cocktails, particularly the communal cocktail we call punch.

More than its country of origin, Batavia Arrack is unique in its makeup too. Part sugar cane and part fermented red rice, this distillate brings a more smoky character to the table than its vegetal close relative, agricole rum. Combined with the sweet honey and plum spirits below, it gives a slightly funky backbone to a great drink for any season.

Arrack of the Killer Bees

1 oz Batavia Arrack van Oosten

½ oz Barenjager

½ oz Averell Damson Gin Liqueur (sub sloe gin if needed)

½ oz fresh lime juice

½ oz cinnamon syrup

2 dashes ginger bitters

Shake all ingredients with ice and strain over fresh 1" ice cubes in a rocks glass. Garnish with a cinnamon stick.

Pisco Volante (left),
Arrack of the Killer Bees

Oh Canada! . . . Please Make Better Whiskies

I've never kept it secret that, in the broad sense, I can't stand Canadian whiskey. I believe I'm not alone in this opinion. The big brands like Windsor, Crown Royal, Black Velvet, Canadian Club . . . they offer so little noteworthy character. I've always regarded these as the toilet wines of the whiskey world.

Canada's spirit regulations don't help. They allow nearly 10% imported spirits and caramel color to be blended with what is usually a very light rye domestic spirit. Renowned for their "smoothness", what little flavor is there usually repels anyone with even remotely discerning taste buds. This is why you really never see Canadian whiskey in cocktails, or at any bar that even distantly cares about its spirit offerings.

Don't get me wrong. I visit Canada as much as I can and would live there for innumerable reasons. And like any spirit category, Canadian whiskies do have some standout brands—JP Wisers, Pike Creek, and Pendleton to name a few. I'd sooner spend my loonies on Gooderham & Worts Four Grain. Canada revived this once major brand using the original 1837 mashbill of corn, rye, wheat and barley.

I like this spirit in a simple "white Manhattan" style mixture. Some jerk already took the name "Toronto" for a pretty insanely good classic cocktail, so you can thank that person for this drink's awkward name. Use google translate if you need the French translation.

East of Etobicoke

2 oz Gooderham & Worts (or substitute Pendleton Rye 12)

½ oz Carpano Bianco

½ oz Genepy des Alpes

2 dashes Runamok Maple Bitters

Stir all ingredients with ice and strain into a chilled coupe glass. Garnish with a Luxardo cherry on a skewer.

Oni the Lonely

The growth of Asian-fusion restaurant bars in my area has helped me warm up to matcha tea cocktails. Even the simplest gin cocktails using this earthy tea taste quite lovely. The powdered form of green tea also gives cocktails a lightly frothy texture without the use of other additives like aquafaba or egg white.

This cocktail not only uses matcha tea and other Japanese ingredients, but shows my fascination with Oni, the demons that inhabit Japanese folklore. These murderous and sometimes cannibalistic creatures lived in many Japanese fairy tales like Momotaro (or "peach boy", hence the peach cordial in this creation). Oni often wielded an iron club called a "kanobo". This term let me playfully pay tribute to cocktails named after famous clubs like the Pegu Club (in an admittedly dark fashion).

Kanobo Club

¾ oz Matcha tea

1.5 oz Lockhouse Sakura Gin (or other cherry blossom gin

½ oz Mathilde Peche cordial

1 oz yuzu juice

2 dashes cherry bitters

Shake all ingredients with ice and strain over a large ice cube in a teacup or rocks glass. Place an edible orchid or other flower on top of the cube.

Waldmeister Uber Alles

Woodruff syrup is so good and unique, this book just demands another cocktail that uses it. It's not just for beer.

The adventurous mixer will find it can also master or tame high proof spirits in a balanced cocktail. In keeping with its literal German roots, this mixture calls for traditional Deutscher spirits. But it can also be made with some easy substitutions. Try a little float of mulled "gluhwein" for a fun holiday twist.

Grun Holle (Green Hell)

½ oz Woodruff Syrup

1 oz Schneider Edelster Aventinus (distilled beer spirit, can be subbed with a light wheat whiskey)

1 oz Asbach Uralt (or other spirit such as St George pear brandy)

1 oz Carpano Dry Vermouth

½ oz gluhwein (optional mulled wine float)

Stir all but gluhwein with ice. Strain over a large format ice cube in a rocks glass. If desired, slowly float gluhwein onto the cube surface using the neck of a bar spoon. Place a single raspberry on top of the ice cube.

Kanobo Club (left), Grun Holle

The Other Corn Liquor

When one mentions corn liquor, it usually brings to mind Mellow Corn or other less eloquent spirits. Let's try the lesser known Mexican Elote spirit today. Nixta Elote or Mexican corn spirit comes from cacahuazintle maize grown in the volcanic soils of Nevado de Toluca. It honors the Mexican craft of nixtamalization—an ancient Mesoamerican cooking technique that derives the deepest aromas and flavors from the corn.

So much did this unique backstory entice me that I had Nixta shipped from another state. Bear in mind that mezcals such as Vago Mezcal Elote exist too, but these will be smoky agave spirits with a hint of roasted corn from a secondary distillation. If you enjoy these flavors, the mezcal works just as well. This mixture joins either base spirit with other flavors native to Mexico.

Joe vs the Volcano

1.5 oz Nixta Elote spirit

½ oz Ancho Reyes Verde

½ oz Agavero or other sweet orange cordial

½ oz brown sugar syrup

¾ oz fresh lime juice

Tajin spice (for glass rim)

Moisten the rim of a tulip or pilsner glass with lime and dip in a dish of Tajin spice. Shake all liquid ingredients with ice and serve on ice in the rimmed glass. Garnish with a fresh poblano pepper and/or lime wheel.

Personality Crisis

The foodie world calls Kalamansi "the Philippine lime". This fascinating citrus fruit wears the vibrant green skin of a lime, but a shape and pulp resembling an orange. And if the packaging doesn't confuse you enough, this tart fruit combines flavors of lime, orange and lemon.

Kalamansi fruit or juice could prove hard to find, but syrup can be found through more cocktail-focused providers.

Manila Fling

¾ oz Kalamansi syrup

½ oz fresh lime juice

1 oz pineapple juice

1 oz Paul Masson Mango Brandy

1 oz Ferrand Dry Orange Curacao

1 oz Porter's Tropical Old Tom Gin

Combine all ingredients with ice in a shaker. Shake contents until chilled and strain over ice in pilsner glass or other tall glass. Garnish with pineapple.

Joe vs Volcano (left), Manila Fling

Sloe Motion

Sloe gin. I've blathered many praises to this spirit previously, perhaps even in this very book. I'm that fucking lazy that I just don't want to confirm it. Seriously, how shiftless is that when I could just run a word search?. . .

The sloe, or a very small plum native to the UK, gave us what I consider England's truly distinctive contribution to the world's spirit palette. Sure, the Dutch invented gin. England basically stole the original recipe, eventually made it drier, and added many more botanicals. But then, they used sweet plums to turn this gin into a lovely liqueur. And rarely will you ever see it coming from any other country than England.

Sloe gin too often gets a bad rap or no rap. The bad rap comes along when you can only find a bottom shelf producer marketed in your area. The bad rap stems from the fact that it's on so few bar shelves, it always appears on the edge of extinction. Even most craft bars use so little that good sloe gins commonly fade away from the drinking public's eye. If a young person even knows what sloe gin is, that person would likely see it as an "old man's drink".

I say to those naysayers—go back to the classic tomes like the Savoy Cocktail Book. Learn about sloe gin, and Amer Picon, and Kronan Swedish Punsch, and all this great shit that still exists, no matter how remote it may seem. Impress your friends. Enjoy and respect your drink, dammit.

Plum Loco

1 oz Plymouth or Hayman's Sloe Gin

1 oz Código 1530 Tequila Rosa

½ oz fresh lime juice

½ oz fresh lemon juice

½ oz ginger syrup

¼ oz honey syrup

Club soda

Shake all ingredients except soda with ice and strain over fresh ice in Collins glass. Top with soda. Garnish with a lime wedge.

Chapter 12: Mr. Bitterness
Cocktails Inspired by Bitters

Surely I rambled on and on about bitters in my first book. I would confirm that but laziness prevails. Seriously, that's sad. A copy is sitting not three feet away from me.

A true cocktail nerd geeks out over bitters. The array of flavors in bitters honestly dwarfs that in the spirits world, if you look hard enough. Simply put, bitters combine "tinctures" or herbs, fruits or other plants extracted into high proof spirit. The base plant often delves into unexpected and exotic territory, like prickly pear, tobacco, or even celery. The other secret herbs in the background just add to the fun.

Bitters also bridge the spirit flavors together in your drink. Just imagine your Manhatatan or Old Fashioned without the bitters. Actually don't. It's just heresy to even think it.

As I start this chapter, I've accumulated a ridiculous arsenal of bitters—impulse buys that just had to be in my home bar because they're so singularly odd. Every drink in this chapter does not yet exist as I type this sentence. Worry not, as they will all get road tested. Just bear in mind that the drinks to come truly owe their existence to the inspiration of one or more types of bitters.

If you don't like bitters, well, we can't be friends anymore. No refunds.

Leaves and Leather

Tobacco bitters struck me as odd upon first discovering them. Then being determined to hoard every flavor of bitters known to humankind, these eventually made it to our home bar. We first tried 18.21 Bitters Havana & Hide Barrel Aged Bitters from Atlanta. And while it does have that whiff of cigar leaf, it also hints at sandalwood, clove and chicory. It's a southern work of art.

I wanted these essences to shine in a spirited stirred cocktail, where they would not get lost among assertive amari or other dark herbal spirits. This drink builds upon Irish whiskey that has been softened by long aging and finishing in sherry barrels, with a supporting cast of lush grape spirits.

Dublin Castle

1.5 oz Bushmill's 10 Year Irish Whiskey

¾ oz Cocchi Americano

¾ oz Martell Cognac

2 dashes 18.21 Havana & Hide Bitters

Add all three spirits to a mixing glass and stir with ice. Strain into a chilled Nick & Nora or classic coupe glass. Drip bitters onto the drink surface. Garnish with a dried star anise.

Blossoms and Barbs

Prickly pears grow on a certain family of cacti in the western hemisphere. And a small handful of producers decided to make bitters with them. These pair best with citrus and tropical fruits, making it easy for a tiki bartender like myself to put them to good use.

Serve it to friends garnished with tropical fruits or flowers. Serve it to enemies garnished with nopales or spiny, barbed cactus leaves. Then you can smugly say, "I've bled for my art, now it's your turn."

Adios, Maria

1 oz papaya juice

2 oz reposado tequila

¾ oz fresh lime juice

½ honey mix syrup

2-3 dashes Seven Stills Prickly Pear Bitters

Shake all but bitters with ice and strain mixture over fresh ice in a highball or Collins glass. Drip bitters onto the drink surface, to taste. Garnish with dried tropical fruits on a bamboo skewer (or cactus pear wheel, if available).

Check your Katana at the Door

I almost regret discovering the Japanese Bitters Co. They only offer five varieties but each one runs about $45 per eyedropper bottle. After much deliberation, I settled on umami, which proved the most unique option. The other options remotely resembled some less exotic bitters, but these will make their way to us as credit card points allow.

The umami bitters remind me of mildly salty miso soup, with a subtle citrus finish. Bearing in mind what chefs recommend for umami pairings, I arrived at the mixture below.

Sushi Girl

2 oz Suntory Toki Japanese Whiskey

¾ oz Yuzu juice (sub lemon if needed)

½ oz maple syrup mix (50/50 dilution)

¼ oz Haku Sakura Cherry Blossom Shoyu

3 dashes Japanese Bitters Co. Umami Bitters

Shake all but bitters with ice and strain over a large format cube in a rocks glass. Drizzle bitters on drink surface. Garnish with dried flower petals.

Sushi Girl (left), Adios Maria

Memphis Soul Stew

I tend to avoid whiskey sours mainly out of laziness. They seem to me the one egg white drink that gets mainstream attention at any above-average cocktail bar. Hence, including one on a menu gets about as many requests as other classics like the Old Fashioned. This amounts to a lot of long and vigorous shaking, which no one on my side of the bar relishes doing. Guests also wait longer to slake their thirst.

Which is why I set out to amp up the whiskey sour with some other unique flavors. This recipe took inspiration from Bitter End's Memphis BBQ Bitters. It also helped me shed light on lesser known Tennessee whiskey, while getting a slight hint of woody smoke. I guess you could call it my liquid tribute to the great early country artists that emigrated or originated in Tennessee like Ernie Ford.

Perhaps cue up Ernest Tubb's "Driving Nails in my Coffin" while drinking this. Listen and you'll know why.

Blue Yodel #9

1.75 oz Nelson's Green Briar Tennessee Sour Mash Whiskey

¼ oz Espadin Mezcal

¾ oz honey mix

1 egg white

2 dashes Bitter End Memphis BBQ Bitters

Shake egg whites vigorously without ice in a shaker tin. Add ice and remaining ingredients, then shake vigorously until blended and frothy. Strain mixture into a coupe glass. Garnish with a lemon peel.

A Tribute to Willie T

Before becoming the beloved cocktail snob you know today, I spent many a year at my father-in-law Bill's dining room table drinking with him and his brother in-law Ray. I'd bring along a six-pack of Guinness Extra Stout, and cringe at the copious amounts of Windsor Canadian, Miller High Life, and Winston cigarettes consumed by those around me.

As much as those vices turned me green, I cherish those weekends. Bill has been one of the kindest and most giving people I've ever known. Getting to chill with him while he and Ray regaled us with tales of bad behavior from days past . . . it just didn't get better.

I offer my tribute to Bill "Willie T" Harnett in the form of this drink. It builds upon some of the few Canadian whiskies I will endorse, while suggesting a hint of tobacco in the background. It's a play on the Old Fashioned, which I think would appeal to everyone around that table way back when.

Sign Painters Union

2 oz Pike Creek or Gooderham & Worts Canadian Whiskey

½ oz rich maple syrup

¼ oz Cointreau

2 dashes 18.21 Havana & Hide bitters (or other comparable tobacco bitters)

Peel of golden apple

Using muddler, lightly press golden apple peel in a mixing glass with syrup and bitters. Add spirits and ice, then stir. Strain mixture over a large ice cube in a rocks glass. Lay a fresh apple peel over the cube.

Barking Mad

Bittercube produces fantastic bitters. When they made root beer bitters, I decided I had to use them in a drink creation, no matter how odd they sounded. As it turned, the sassafras bark, anise and dandelion elements paired well with barrel-aged spirits and even tiki drinks, while lending a hint of earthiness. I think this drink brings all of the perfect pairings for these slightly gingery bitters into one glass. It's a simple drink that lets the bitters shine through.

The Stranger

- 1.5 oz dark aged rum
- ½ oz cinnamon syrup
- ¾ oz lemon juice
- ½ oz Bitter Truth Apricot cordial
- 4 dashes Bittercube Root Beer Bitters

Combine all ingredients with ice in a shaker. Shake contents until chilled and strain over ice in pilsner glass or other tall glass. Garnish with cinnamon stick or rocky candy stick.

Stranger (left), Adios Maria

A Winter's Tale

This boils down to a confession that I was completely unfamiliar with winter melon before Bittermen's developed bitters from it. It's not even a melon; it's an Asian vegetable commonly called ash gourd. And being that they come from the same plant family as cucumbers, zucchini and pumpkins, the flesh of the plant stays pretty bland throughout it's oddly long shelf life of 3-4 months. It's harvested in summer but normally stored for consumption in winter, when its skin sheds fine hairlike fibers that reveal it's still not ripe.

Why would such an oddball plant inspire a singular style of bitters? When timed and handled just right, apparently it brings out tart berry and cucumber flavors that suit gin and other clear spirits really well. In fact these bitters bring some serious razzle-dazzle to an otherwise garden variety gin and tonic.

In that spirit, this drink builds upon gin and other clean flavors that let the bitters shine through.

Sink or Swim

1.5 oz Aviation Gin

½ oz Bianco Vermouth

½ oz Pierre Ferrand Dry Curacao

2 dashes Bittermen's Winter Melon Bitters

1 drop Fee Brothers Hibiscus Water

Combine all ingredients except curacao with ice in a mixing glass. Stir until ice level drops and mixture is chilled. Strain into a chilled coupe. Slowly pour curacao into glass to sink the spirit to the bottom.

Lucky 13: The Lazy Chapter

Honestly I planned to stop at Chapter 12. Then I thought it would be fun to have my favorite number 13. So with colossal laziness, I share the fruits of two separate cocktail pop-ups I hosted during my humble career: a daiquiri night, and a holiday season pop-up based on rum and gin drinks.

The Daiquiri Factory: Easy Spins on Perfection

This is a short soliloquy to my favorite three-ingredient classic—the Daiquiri.

Early in my bartending history, a good friend in the industry told me the classic daiquiri is the perfect cocktail. It can be made quickly. It's always good. And it lets you enjoy the essences of any rum with the two most common ingredients in any cocktail bar.

I'm quite inclined to agree. On so many occasions, I enter a tiki bar with eyes on the most intricate heritage tropical cocktails. Half the time I'll scan the menu for five minutes before settling on a classic daiquiri. If my eyes lock on a new rum at the back bar first, I usually default to a daiquiri made with said rum.

A good friend in the industry hosted a pop-up on behalf of my bar in the summer of 2022, while we transitioned into a new location. We'd done pop-ups at other bars around the same time that featured several complex tiki drinks. Perhaps coordinating these drinks between several bars over a number of months weighed me down. By the time we approached this final pop-up, we decided to streamline this event into several expressions of the perfect rum classic.

We deemed the event "The Daiquiri Factory". One of the featured drinks was the Devil's Daiquiri, developed a few years before my first book but belatedly included in the Hot Mess chapter of this book. The menu included four other daiquiri variations that I share with you here. These all employ spirits included in my first book as well.

Serve them to friends. Half of them will expect a sickly sweet frozen drink in a silly glass. Fuck, you'd be surprised how many bartenders don't know how to make one.

Danish Daiquiri

1 oz Plantation 3 Star Rum

0.5 oz Norden Aquavit

0.5 oz Elderflower cordial

0.75 oz fresh lime juice

0.75 oz demerara simple syrup

Dynastic Daiquiri

1 oz Plantation 3 Star Rum

0.5 oz Giffard Lychi-Li

0.5 oz Plum Wine

0.75 oz fresh lime juice

0.75 oz demerara simple syrup

Double Funk Daiquiri

1 oz Smith & Cross Rum

1 oz Wray & Nephew Overproof Rum

0.75 oz fresh lime juice

0.75 oz demerara simple syrup

2 dashes Bittermen's Elemakule Tiki Bitters

Del Mar Daiquiri

1 oz Cazadores Reposado

1 oz Doctor Bird Pineapple Rum

0.75 oz fresh lime juice

0.75 oz demerara simple

2 dashes Angostura Cocoa Bitters

For any of these variations, shake all ingredients with ice and strain into a chilled coupe glass. Float a thin lime wheel on the surface of the drink.

Mele Kalikimaka—A Dose of Holiday Rumbullion

Oddly I wish I could hibernate from mid-November through December 30 every year. Strong drink gets me through those six tormenting weeks since a voluntary coma cannot. But oddly, the traditional flavors of the season appeal to me more than most. And it actually helps legitimize the use of cranberry beyond its classic pairing with a certain flavorless, odorless and colorless spirit.

For several ongoing seasons, my bar has paired up with Pussers Rum for a holiday cocktail program. We run some holiday riffs, but also these signature cocktails. You don't have to like the holiday to enjoy these drinks. So cue up Fear's Fuck Christmas on 45 and sip responsibly.

Nativity Strength

0.5 oz lime

1 oz Cranberry juice

2 oz fresh orange juice

0.75 oz cinnamon syrup

2 oz Pussers Gunpowder Rum

Shake all ingredients and serve over ice in a Mai Tai glass. Garnish with lime, mint and cinnamon stick.

North Pole Bunker Buster

0.5 oz Nux Alpina

1 oz. Pussers Rum

0.75 oz. lemon juice

0.5 oz. Rittenhouse Rye

0.5 oz. orgeat

0.25 oz. East India Solera Sherry

1 teaspoon cinnamon syrup

3 dashes of Angostura bitters

Combine all ingredients and whip shake with three ice cubes. Pour into a glass over crushed ice and garnish with a lemon wheel, mint, and bitters.

Silent Night, Deadly Night

1 oz Pussers Gunpowder Rum

0.5 oz Macchu Pisco

1 oz Silver rum

0.5 oz Grapefruit juice

0.5 oz cinnamon syrup

0.5 oz falernum

2 dashes Crude Tiki 500 Bitters

Shake all ingredients with ice and strain into a chilled coupe glass. Garnish with a single mint leaf.

Regaling on Remand

1 oz Pussers Rum

1 oz Pussers Gunpowder Rum

0.25 oz Bitter Truth Allspice Dram

0.5 turbinado simple syrup

0.75 lime

Shake and double strain into a chilled coupe glass. Garnish with grated cinnamon.

Uhane Hau'oli (Holiday Spirit)

1.5 oz Fifty Pounds Gin

0.5 oz Cherry Heering

0.5 oz Benedictine

0.5 oz Giffard Pamplemousse

0.25 oz orgeat

0.75 oz lime

2 dashes spiced cherry bitters

Club soda to top

Shake all ingredients with ice and serve over ice in a Collins glass. Top with a splash of soda water. Garnish with a skewered grapefruit peel and cherry.

www.ingramcontent.com/pod-product-compliance
Lightning Source LLC
Chambersburg PA
CBHW060803150426
42813CB00059B/2879